OPPORTUNITIES IN
AEROSPACE
CAREERS

Wallace R. Maples

Foreword by
Louis Smith
President
Future Aviation Professionals of America (FAPA)

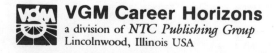 **VGM Career Horizons**
a division of *NTC Publishing Group*
Lincolnwood, Illinois USA

Cover Photo Credits:
Front cover: upper left, General Electric photo;
upper right and lower left, photos courtesy of
Delta Airlines, Inc.; lower right, NASA photo.
Back Cover: upper left and lower right, NASA
photos; upper right, Air France photo; lower
left, AVCO Textron Aerostructures photo.

Library of Congress Cataloging-in-Publication Data

Maples, Wallace, 1935—
    Opportunities in aerospace careers / Wallace R. Maples

        p. cm — (VGM opportunities series)
    ISBN 0-8442-8650-8 : $12.95.—ISBN 0-8442-8651-6 (pbk.) : $9.95
        1. Aerospace industries—Vocational guidance. 2. Aeronautics—
Vocational guidance. I. Title. II. Series.
HD9711.5.A2M36 1990
629.1'023'73—dc20   90-39889
                                                                CIP

Published by VGM Career Horizons, a division of NTC Publishing Group.
©1991 by NTC Publishing Group, 4255 West Touhy Avenue,
Lincolnwood (Chicago), Illinois 60646-1975 U.S.A.
Manufactured in the United States of America.

0 1 2 3 4 5 6 7 8 9 VP 9 8 7 6 5 4 3 2 1

ABOUT THE AUTHOR

Dr. Wallace R. Maples is currently professor of aviation and chair of the aerospace department of Middle Tennessee State University. Originally from Lenoir City, Tennessee, Maples' first aviation experience was as an aviation mechanic with the United States Army's Third Infantry Division Combat Aviation Company at Fort Benning, Georgia. While working in that capacity, he also took flight lessons.

After serving a tour in the army, Maples lived in southern California, where he parachuted with the Southern California Skydivers and worked in the early space instrumentation division of Bourns Laboratories. He continued to take flying lessons in Riverside, California.

The need for additional education prompted Maples to return to college. He received his bachelor's degree from Middle Tennessee State College, his master's degree from the University of Tennessee, and his doctorate from Indiana University. He also completed the private and commercial flight certificates.

In recent years, he has directed numerous aerospace education workshops for teachers and international workshops in 45 countries, has assisted with National Aeronautic and Space Administration (NASA) seminars during several space shuttle launches, and is currently on the board of trustees of the University Aviation Association. He also has assisted with airline training programs and served as chair of the Civil Air Patrol's National Aerospace Education Committee and president of the Tennessee Aerospace Education Association.

ACKNOWLEDGMENTS

It is impossible to compile such a gathering of facts, impressions, statistics, and information about broad career fields without the support of many people and numerous organizations. Not to recognize and thank them would be unconscionable.

The writer is clearly indebted to the following organizations for providing recent statistics on salaries, requirements for employment, and the numbers of people needed in the industry: Future Aviation Professionals of America (FAPA), National Business Aircraft Association (NBAA), Academic Resources, Inc., National Aeronautics and Space Administration (NASA), American Airlines, Inc., the General Aviation Manufacturers Association, and the Federal Aviation Administration (FAA).

At the risk of omitting someone who has made a significant contribution, the following people are recognized for contributing time, effort, and ideas: Dr. Michael Schukert, Dr. Peggy Baty, Stan Smartt, Bill Herrick, Lynn Crane, Sandra Burton, Chris Walsh, Buck Davis, Dr. Rem Schuil, Brett Fulford, A. Scott Crossfield, Alex Evans, Charles Ahlstrand, and the aerospace faculty of Middle Tennessee State University.

To those who assisted and encouraged my entry into aerospace: Dr. Bealer Smotherman, Jack Sorenson, Dr. Merv Strickler, H. Miller Lanier, Dr. Ralph White, and Randall Wood.

Finally, with special thanks to my wife Carolyn, my three sons Greg, Steve, and Bill, and my mother Mary G. Maples, who 'thought I could.'

FOREWORD

Air and space travel, concepts which only became reality in this century, today provide a wealth of opportunity for those entering the field as a career choice. As we look to a new century, those opportunities look even greater for the future.

Airlines, airports, manufacturers, governments, military and space programs—all will require numerous trained and qualified personnel in order to compete in tomorrow's world markets. You may very well be one of those people.

As examples of the impending need for skilled aviation professionals, Future Aviation Professionals of America (FAPA) projects that in the next decade alone, U.S. airlines will hire 52,000 to 62,000 pilots, 100,000 flight attendants, and 64,000 maintenance and avionics technicians. These numbers do not even begin to approach the numbers needed in airline support personnel and nonairline aviation and aerospace operations.

The opportunities are numerous, varied, lucrative, and exciting. If, after reading this book, you decide that an aviation/aerospace career is for you, you will begin a lifelong discovery of the people, technology and the mysteries of the skies that make the field what it is today, and what it will be tomorrow. I'm sure you will find the experience a rewarding one.

Louis Smith
President
Future Aviation Professionals of America (FAPA)

CONTENTS

CHAPTER 1

DEFINITION AND HISTORY
OF AEROSPACE

Aerospace. You've heard the word, but what does it mean? The term combines *aero*, from *aeronautics*, referring to flight within the atmosphere, and *space*, signifying flight beyond the atmosphere. However, it really isn't quite so simple, because scientists have not agreed upon where that separation occurs. It is probably more proper to consider the space above us as gradually changing in terms of supporting life without the aid of life-support equipment. Operations within that space above us provide the widest variety of career opportunities of almost any field of endeavor.

A full range of skill, training, and education is necessary to conceive, develop, build, pilot, and maintain the aircraft that fly above us. Aeronautical and astronautical engineers, machinists, managers, pilots, flight attendants, maintenance and avionics technicians, air traffic controllers, and astronauts are among the people employed in the hundreds of careers available in aerospace.

This guide will assist you in exploring the myriad of jobs available to you in aerospace. The chapters will be devoted to exploring the workplace and therein the types of jobs found within the different workplaces. You will learn what level of education is required, the working conditions within the industry, salaries earned by skilled workers and professionals, and what the job outlook is for the portion of the industry that excites you.

EDUCATION VERSUS TRAINING

Several of the career fields in aerospace require the highest of educational levels, such as a doctorate in engineering, physics, or some other physical science. For such careers, you can anticipate a minimum of seven years of college, with two to three degrees earned on the road to success. On the other hand, there are some aerospace careers for high school graduates that require no college, but rather some specialized training, yet they may result in greater earninhgs than those of a person who has three college degrees. The choice between education and training depends largely upon your career goals and somewhat will reflect a difference between what you may *know* and what you can *do*.

Education

Education focuses on what you know. It involves broad-based learning, which tends to urge the learner to sample many fields of knowledge, concentrating in the latter stages on one specific field, such as physics or engineering. Education prepares you more for the future in general—for developing, designing, and reordering what now exists and for coming up with new knowledge, to create or improve the technology with which everyone must work.

Training

Training involves something you do. This may be a natural aptitude in mechanics, which allows you to work on jet engines or aircraft radios. Or it may involve a very different skill which helps you to control numerous airplanes within a finite airspace—sight unseen. Training prepares you for exceptional performance in a skilled position.

Making Your Own Choice

Education tends to teach a variety of knowledge, including alternative behaviors and ways of thinking, thus making people different in terms of how that knowledge is applied. Training tends to teach a common skill, making people more alike in what they do. The significance of this information for *you* involves what you want from a job or career. Do you wish to learn a skill quickly, which will allow you to earn a comfortable living until retirement, performing essentially the same tasks on a routine basis? Or do you wish to invest several years within formal education, learning the theoretical, abstract, and conceptual stages of a discipline? Education not only leads to essentially more creative positions, but frequently leads to management positions in a career field. Though people may also rise to management levels from skilled positions and enjoy some freedom of expression, they are more likely to feel under pressure to perform beyond their educational preparation. Therefore, college education is recommended if you have managerial aspirations.

The aerospace industry, perhaps more so than any other industry, utilizes virtually every trade, skill, profession, and discipline of study known in modern times. Medical doctors, lawyers, analysts, engineers, accountants, finance specialists, and marketing personnel are but a few of the professionals who may work within aerospace. Skilled craftworkers such as machinists, sheet metal workers, welders, carpenters, and pipefitters may also be employed within aerospace. Nonskilled employees such as typists, drivers, receptionists, and building maintenance workers are needed within aerospace as well. Regardless of your education or training background, you may find a place among the many positions in aerospace.

In addition to the many general skills and professions utilized by aerospace firms, there are abundant aerospace-specific positions available. Aerospace must have pilots, aircraft maintenance technicians, air traffic controllers, flight dispatchers, reservationists, avionics technicians, and safety inspectors, to name a few. We'll learn about all of these positions as we explore the fascinating aerospace world in which we live.

HISTORY OF FLIGHT

The desire to fly has been a part of human nature throughout recorded history. Cave drawings, which are millions of years old, depict flight. Greek and Roman mythology tell a story of a father and son, Daedalus and Icarus, who supposedly escaped an island prison by gluing feathers on their body and flying away. Chinese legends of some 4,000 years ago allow us a glimpse into the desires of those who would fly. In fact, the Chinese invented several items, such as kites and gunpowder, that could make flight possible.

We all know of Leonardo da Vinci's Renaissance drawings of the ornithopter, the parachute, and what we have come to know as the helicopter. Some believe he may have flown models of these flying machines.

The Montgolfier brothers of France were the first to launch live passengers into the ''wild blue yonder,'' at least as far as we know. They had developed the hot air balloon, and in a demonstration for King Louis XVI and Marie Antoinette, sent aloft a rooster, a duck, and a sheep on Sept. 19, 1783. Just two months later, they sent the first humans into the atmosphere. The world of flight began!

It would be some 120 years later before the Wright brothers of Dayton, Ohio, would launch the first powered, controlled flight of a heavier-than-air vehicle. Orville Wright flew for 12 seconds and traveled 120 feet on Dec. 17, 1903, at Kitty Hawk, North Carolina. The entire length of that historic flight could take place inside some of today's cargo planes. It was very important, however, as it set the tone for future flight, in addition to proving that flight could take place. Wouldn't it be great to bring the Wright brothers back to see what they created? Imagine, if you will, that for thousands of years of recorded history, we did not fly. Suddenly, within the span of one lifetime, we are sending people to the moon at speeds in excess of 20,000 miles per hour. What a tremendous leap in technology. What a wonderful period of history for you to be alive and to be able to contribute to the development of aerospace.

CHAPTER 2

AIRLINES

The major airlines must utilize the broadest talent pool available in the entire aerospace industry. There is practically no skill, profession, or trade group that is not in some way represented within a large airline. The airlines hire pilots, flight attendants, lawyers, real estate specialists, analysts, financial planners, medical personnel, accountants, mechanics, managers of all descriptions, baggage handlers, engineers, and chefs. The list is nearly endless.

The major U.S. airlines have been called by various names since their humble beginnings during the 1920s. They have been known as "trunk" carriers, major air carriers, airlines, intercity air transports, and domestic air carriers, to name a few. Today the airlines are divided into three categories on the basis of their annual gross earnings:

1. Major carriers: earn in excess of $1 billion yearly.
2. National carriers: earn between $100 million and $1 billion yearly.
3. Regional carriers: earn less than $100 million yearly.

Regional carriers are further divided into three categories of large, medium, and small carriers. It is with the regional carriers that many people find entry-level positions. They then proceed to work their way up within the organization or move to larger carriers when they have achieved appropriate experience.

Major airlines normally pay the highest wages and salaries, and frequently offer the better benefits. They also offer an additional *"perk"* or *perquisite*—that is, a benefit given in addition to salary, that makes an airline job among the most competitive in the industry: free flights to their employees and to the immediate families of their employees. The number of flights an employee may obtain within a given year and the family members who qualify will vary greatly among the airlines. Often the length of time with the employer will affect the number of flights. *Domestic carriers,* meaning airlines that are based within the United States, that also have international routes will allow employees a certain number of flights to foreign countries as well. One can see that if an airline allows the wife or husband, all children, father and mother, and even brothers and sisters to fly virtually free, it adds to people's desire to work for that airline.

Additional perks that some airlines offer employees are found in the form of ownership or cooperative arrangements with major hotels, resorts, and car rental agencies. When an airline employee takes advantage of the free flights to distant cities, she or he may also receive dramatic discounts on accommodations and ground transportation. All of these factors must be considered when you review the salary for the job. Several thousand dollars per year in cost savings from perks can be added to the already excellent value of the base salary received. At the present time, these perks are relatively free of income tax. How long that will continue remains to be seen!

AIRLINE ORGANIZATIONAL STRUCTURE

To fully understand where you may work within an airline, it is necessary to look briefly at the organizational structure of a major airline. This will allow you to properly prepare yourself for the job you desire and also to understand where you will be working within the structure.

The major airlines generally are divided into at least four categories:

1. Operations: day-to-day functions of putting planes into the air, with job categories like pilot, flight attendant, and flight dispatcher.
2. Maintenance: daily checks on airplanes to major over-haul of airframe and engines, including avionics, fuel-ing, and routine items like changing tires.
3. Marketing: may include everything from sales to fore-casting next year's passenger load, to advertising, res-ervations, and food services.
4. Finance: includes purchasing, auditing, investment, borrowing capital funds, and planning property acqui-sition.

It is obvious that many functions are not included in the outline. You may obtain books from several sources which will afford a more in-depth look at the organization of airlines, so that you may become more familiar with the department in which you wish to work. Appendix A lists major airline corporate addresses. Man-agement functions occur in all airline divisions and within a *line and staff* framework, *line* referring to direct command and deci-sion-making functions, and *staff* having to do with support ser-vices. It is difficult to determine by title alone whether a particular manager is considered in a line function or a staff position.

Enough about airline organization. You want to find out about the many specific jobs airlines offer. Let us first consider those that require very specialized training and education, plus certifi-cation by the Federal Aviation Administration (FAA).

AIRLINE PILOT

Perhaps the most exotic, romantic, and debonair position to which one may aspire today is that of the airline pilot. The word *pilot* conjures up glamorous images of being in charge, of making life-and-death decisions in a split second, and of exotic travel to faraway places. All of these attributes may be true at times. However, there is more truth to be found in a rather routine day of driving to the airport, looking over weather charts, going aboard the airplane, running through a checklist, starting engines, taxiing out for takeoff, and flying without incident to another airport some two to four hours away. Piloting is a way of earning a living, a rather good one for sure, but one with routine, consistent, and often boring work, not unlike jobs in other fields.

The major airline pilot has paid his or her dues well before assuming command of a Boeing 747 with 400 passengers aboard. The pilot usually either began flying in general aviation or was trained in the military and has already logged hundreds of hours in the air.

Education

The major air carrier pilot going into this career today will have a bachelor's degree from an accredited university. While this was not the case for many current captains when they came into the airlines, it is the exception today for one to be hired without a college degree. For example, the Future Aviation Professionals of America (FAPA) organization reported that during the first six months of 1989, more than 90 percent of the new hires at 6 of the 12 major carriers had four years or more of college. At another 4 of the 12 carriers, 85 percent of the new hires had four years or more of college. If you aspire to rise to the level of a pilot with the major airlines, be aware that your competition probably has a college degree.

Some pilots will continue to be hired without a college degree. However, all scheduled carriers will give preference to those with a degree. As the pilot crunch becomes more severe, airlines will become less concerned about several factors, education among them. They will be more concerned with getting their planes from point A to point Z. In this regard, there are several good schools, community colleges, and private fixed base operators that will provide excellent flight training.

Certification

Pilots in training for future commercial flight positions will normally obtain a series of certificates, beginning with the private pilot certificate and continuing through the instrument rating, the commercial certificate, the multiengine rating, and the air transport pilot (ATP) certificate, which is the "Ph.D." of pilot certificates. Current FAA regulations allow a person to achieve the private certificate in 35 flight hours, the commercial and instrument in 190 hours and the air transport certificate in 1,500 hours. All of this assumes that the individual has had the proper instruction, passed written examinations and flight checks, and has the appropriate hours of night, instrument, cross-country, and solo flight. According to FAPA, more than two-thirds of all major airline pilot hires in 1988 had the ATP certificate. Those who did not were, for the most part, military pilots.

Airline pilots will continue to learn on-the-job, will go back for recurrent training frequently, will keep up with the literature and will progress into more complex and larger aircraft until they reach the pinnacle of success.

About every 10 to 15 years, a new generation of air carrier aircraft comes along, which completely revolutionizes the industry. The most recent evidence of this are Boeing's 757 and 767, and the Airbus A-340. These aircraft are capable of taxiing onto the runway, taking off, flying a complex course of several direction and altitude changes, landing, and taxiing off the runway—without the pilot ever touching the controls! The pilot may program the onboard computers prior to leaving the gate, should an automated flight be desired.

Working Conditions

The airline pilot may not fly in excess of 85 hours per month or 1,000 hours per year, according to FAA regulations. Many people confuse that with the total work load of a pilot. Nothing could be further from the truth. The pilot spends countless hours in the dispatch office planning trips, hours commuting to work from as far away as several hundred miles, working on reports, briefing crews, attending flight recurrent training or management schools, and performing other duties as designated by the company. Many pilots represent their companies in public speaking engagements, on committees for pilot welfare, and on national committees that work toward the enhancement of flight safety. Add to this the major layovers required of international and long-route domestic flights, and you can see that the pilot is quite busy over long periods of time.

Of course, the major part of the profession involves what every pilot loves the most: flying. The pilot spent thousands of dollars and countless hours of preparation getting to the cockpit and thereby deserves all of the rewards and respect that accrue to the position.

Members of ethnic minorities and women were excluded from the cockpits of the major carriers for years, despite the contributions they made to popularizing flight. Such is not the case today. Although fewer than 1 percent of current airline pilots are black, this figure is likely to increase in the coming decades as more blacks enter flight training programs. American Airlines in 1964 voluntarily hired the first black pilot to be employed by a major carrier.

Female pilots have been hired by the airlines in increasing numbers only since 1973, when Emily Warner was hired by the regional carrier Frontier Airlines. It was a tough struggle for her and one she was not sure she would ever win. When she was hired, she had a total of 7,000 hours of flying time. The first woman hired by a major carrier was Bonnie Tiburzi, hired by American Airlines in 1973. In addition to being an excellent pilot, she is also a model who has appeared in several national magazines.

The struggle by women to occupy equal status with men in the cockpit traces from 1911, when Harriet Quimby became the first American woman to earn a pilot certificate. Some interesting stories of the trials and tribulations of female pilots are included in the bibliography in Appendix B at the back of this book.

Salary

Earnings for airline pilots who fly with the major carriers are among the highest salaried jobs in America. It has been said that the average earnings of major airline pilots are greater than the average for medical doctors. If not, it must surely approach such earnings.

A pilot with the major airlines, with 10 years of service, earns an average of $85,284 per year, plus benefits and *per diem*—living expenses when away from the crew base, calculated at an average rate of $1.50 per hour. One must realize that this is an average. Salaries vary considerably among even the major carriers. Some have no union to negotiate wage and working conditions contracts. Some have a relatively new B Scale entering wage that may not reach parity with other pilots for nine years or more.

Salaries for pilots with national air carriers and the various levels of regional carriers will vary much more than with the major airlines. The first officer with a national airline will average $21,036 to start. For a captain, the maximum average is $79,860. One can anticipate a beginning salary with the commuter (small regional) airline to be in the vicinity of $14,664 per year, rising to $34,163 for a captain. These are average salaries. Different airlines will be above or below these representative figures. The turnover rate with the regional carriers is very high, with some having as much as a 120 percent turnover per year. This likely will stabilize by the mid-1990s, due to consolidation of airlines and the buyout of smaller regionals by the major carriers.

Many factors must be considered when comparing careers, especially where salary is a major factor. In addition to the length of time one is with an airline, there are other ingredients that make up the salary recipe. These other items include type of aircraft flown, whether the job is on domestic or international routes, and whether it is with a unionized airline, along with considerations for over-water, night, and holiday flights. Thus, the salary of an airline captain whom you may personally know could be tens of thousands of dollars on either side of the average.

In fact, some pilots for small airlines fly for salaries below the poverty level in order to build precious flight time and gain experience that will help them progress to the larger carriers. One way to understand the wide variation in salaries is to look at the *range* as well as the average. The range takes into consideration the high and the low for a given position. FAPA figures show that the range for major airline captains making the maximum base salary varies from a low of $71,000 to a high of $166,548. Another factor to consider when looking at salaries is whether the salary is earned or is based only on the pay scale. Earned salaries tend to be higher. It is generally felt that many captains earn over

$200,000 per year, although their base salary is considerably lower.

Employment Outlook

So you say, "OK, great salary and working conditions, but what are my chances of finding employment as a pilot?" Actually, never better. Depending upon the source of information, estimates of civilian pilot needs for the 1990s are given at between 52,000 and 108,000. The majority of major carriers are 'very senior' in pilot personnel, meaning that older pilots dominate the ranks. Some carriers will lose fully 60 percent of their pilots by the year 2000. They will not only have to replace retiring pilots, but they will also have to add pilots to fly the billions of dollars worth of aircraft currently on order. Many of these aircraft are not replacements, they are additions to be flown on expanded routes.

The Bottom Line

Flying for the scheduled airlines can provide an excellent lifestyle. In fact, a major airline executive recently commented that being a pilot is not a career at all, it is a way of life. The pay is great, the travel is extensive, and the working conditions are generally excellent. The employment opportunities, at least for the next 10 years, seem superb.

The major disadvantage of becoming a pilot is the cost for the various certificates needed, the amount of dues-paying time to qualify for airline employment, and the fact that pilots must retire at age 60, regardless of whether they wish to or not. And while pilots may obtain free flights for family members, the nature of their job nevertheless requires a fair amount of time away from home and family.

MAINTENANCE TECHNICIAN

Perhaps the second-greatest need in the aerospace field today is for maintenance personnel. Need has to do with the lack of availability of workers in skilled areas for which an extended amount of time or formal schooling is required. The maintenance technician is the backbone of the airline. Without the technician, the airplane does not fly, and the remaining airline employees are out of work. Safety is foremost in the mind of everyone who works for an airline. President Robert Crandall of American Airlines has indicated that he feels personally responsible for safety within American. When the head of any corporation takes responsibility for any attribute or characteristic of that company, one can be assured that it is on the mind of everyone else within the company.

The technician in today's aerospace environment is confronting a very different setting than those who came before. The technology has changed by quantum leaps within a very short period. Much of the change came about with the introduction of the jet airplane in commercial service. The first U.S. airline to fly a pure jet was National Airlines in 1958. Yet it took several years to replace the piston engine, even in the airlines. Today we not only have the jet, but we also have increasingly more complicated engines, much larger engines, and the new glass cockpit. All of the analog instrument technology is being replaced by a cathode ray tube (CRT), a small, television-type screen. The engine instruments in which the pilot once placed so much faith now may not appear unless the pilot calls them up, or the computer that monitors the engines wishes to alert the pilot to a problem. Technicians not only confront new instrumentation and engines, but also composite materials being utilized in place of all metal structures. Anticipated changes are expected to be even greater in the foreseeable future.

Education

The aircraft maintenace technician—or mechanic, as he or she may be referred to in some areas—comes to that trade by several routes. The three main ways to become a technician are:

1. By experience, working under the guidance of a certified technician.
2. By formal training in a school certified by the FAA.
3. By experience and training while serving in the military, with subsequent certification by the FAA.

Whichever you choose, the target to shoot for is FAA certification as an airframe and power plant technician. If you come to such certification via experience, you must spend a minimum of 18 months of full time work in each specialty, under the direction of one or more certified technicians. You may choose to attend a formal school. This may be a vocational school, one assocated with a high school, an associate degree program, or a maintenance management program, wherein one can earn both the bachelor's degree and the requisite certificates. The school must be an FAA-certified maintenance technician school. Another method of obtaining education is through a technical school operated by a branch of the military and by working in that area during military service.

Certification

The maintenance technician must have either an airframe certificate or a power plant certificate, or both. The only exception to this is to work in a certified repair station in a given specialty, such as welding, metal forming, or engine repair. The technician may obtain a repair certificate after at least 18 months of practical experience in the duties of the specific job for which he or she is employed.

The airframe and power plant certificate, also called the A&P, is awarded by the FAA when the successful applicant has been recommended by either the school, the repair station, or the technician under which the person has apprenticed, or by presenting military documentation of schooling, plus practical experience. The applicant must, in addition to experience and schooling, take written, oral, and practical examinations given by the FAA or by a designated examiner. There are no shortcuts to success.

After a maintenance technician with an A&P works for some time in the field, he or she probably will wish to achieve the next level of certification. This is called the inspector authorization (IA) and may be given to the A&P technician upon application to the local FAA office. The technician must be an experienced person, must be capable of effective supervision of colleagues, and must have the availability of an up-to-date technical library of airworthiness directives and other FAA data.

Working Conditions

The maintenance technician works in a variety of places, even within an airline. If you like to work under pressure, with rarely a dull moment, working on the line at the many airports served by your airline is the place to be. The technician will often make rapid repairs, change tires, replace instruments, or make decisions about grounding the plane—that is, not allowing it to continue to fly without repairs that may be too extensive to maintain that airplane's schedule.

The technician has the best of technology to assist in making decisions about a particular airplane. If the pilot calls ahead that she or he is encountering a problem, the technician goes directly to the computer, which is usually in contact with the airline's maintenance base. The technician calls up the record of the specific airplane, which lists everything done on that individual plane since it was purchased. The technician usually will call up only the information for the most recent week or the past couple of days. This information helps the technician determine what the problem might be. He or she may also consult maintenance manuals on this specific type of airplane and discuss the problem with other technicians. The computer will not only assist in making a decision, but will also show whether the necessary parts are available at the airport. If not, the technician can have the parts delivered.

When the airplane arrives, the technician further analyzes the problem and makes a decision as to what is needed. One of the disadvantages of working as a technician at the airport is weather. The airplane may be too large to push into a hangar, so the technician often works outside. The job may be in Chicago in January, with winds of 40 miles per hour and subzero temperatures that cut to the bone. Or it may be in El Paso in July, with even stronger winds and temperatures hovering around 100 degrees Fahrenheit. Of course, it might be in New Orleans in April and be just perfect.

There are basically six types of maintenance checks that are accomplished on an airplane. Normally only two of these are completed without a hangar and specialized equipment. If you are working at a maintenance or overhaul base, you will be working with hundreds of other technicians and likely will be doing shift work, as these bases work around the clock. One of the major carriers, which already has a huge maintenance base, is adding another at a cost of some $400 million. The new facility will employ 2,500 technicians immediately and will grow to 4,500 technicians. No small operation this maintenance business.

Aside from airlines, the maintenance technician will find employment with the major airframe and engine manufacturers, the military, and within general aviation. These areas of employment are covered in other chapters of this book.

Salary

The salary levels of the maintenance technician vary with experience, certification, level of responsibility, and geographic region of the nation, as well as with the type of company for which the technician works. Among the airlines, the major carriers pay the highest average salary. In 1989, the highest maximum average for a technician was $23.32 per hour. The average maximum for all major carriers was $20.48, according to FAPA. Table 2.1 gives some examples of salary levels for maintenance technicians.

Table 2.1
Maintenance Technician Salaries

Level of Carrier	Beginning	Maximum
Major Airline	$13.57	$20.48
National	$11.86	$17.45
Turbojet	$10.86	$14.85
Regional	$ 8.35	$13.16
Helicopter	$ 9.17	$15.85

Source: Future Aviation Professionals of America (FAPA)

Employment Outlook

Forecasts from the FAA, FAPA, and the Federal Bureau of Labor indicate an excellent future for the technician. Scheduled airlines and corporation aviation employ approximately 61,000 technicians. The airlines will continue to be the source of most jobs, due to staff retirement and to additional equipment placed on the line. The hiring rate for the airlines alone comes to 10,000 to 11,000 workers per year. It is estimated that the shortfall in trained technicians may approach 40,000 during the 1990s.

The prospects for moving into supervisory positions also look bright. A recent survey of *Journal of Aviation Equipment Mainte-nance* readers, who are generally management personnel, indi-cated that the typical manager was 41 years old and had worked

in aircraft maintenance for 15 years, with 64 percent of the respondents supervising fewer than 15 persons. Nearly half the respondents had completed a college level education.

The Bottom Line

The long-term job outlook for maintenace technicians is great. The pay is increasing at approximately 5 percent per year, adjusted for inflation, and the jobs are to be found almost anywhere there is an airport with scheduled air carrier service. Job prospects are best at the large domiciles of major carriers. However, there are many other opportunities for technicians outside the airlines, as will be explained in upcoming chapters. If you are good with your hands, like mechanical challenges, and are adept at reading and interpreting what you read, a maintenance technician's career could be the correct choice for you.

RESERVATION SALES AGENT

Airline reservations may be made with a travel agency or directly with the airline. Although the majority of reservations are made through a travel agency, all airlines of any size will have a reservations system, or they will contract with a larger airline to handle reservations on their behalf.

Reservations made directly with the airline may be accomplished by phone or by walking into one of a variety of ticket offices operated by the airline. We are probably most familiar with reservations made by phone or by purchasing our tickets at the airport. Airlines, depending upon their size and desired visibility, may have a downtown city ticket office (CTO) or may share a ticket office with other airlines in large hotels or in business districts. They may also have a ticket office located at large

military bases, referred to as a joint airline military ticket office (JAMTO), usually staffed by agents from several carriers. Wherever the traveler purchases the airline ticket, contact for the reservation itself was probably made by phone. Thus, we need to consider the reservation sales agent in our discussion of various airline careers.

Education

The reservation sales agent is not required to have any specific level of education beyond high school. However, the airline desires as highly educated a person as possible. While the agent is not seen by the customer, the agent may be the first contact between the airline and a customer, who is referred to as a *client* in the industry. The agent "becomes" the airline to the client Speed, efficiency, courtesy, and providing what the client wants arc all sales techniques that the experienced agent provides. While education cannot guarantee skill in these techniques, it usually can enhance the probability of the agent providing a better service. Airline reservation sales agents work not only with clients, but also in some instances with travel agents who call on behalf of their clients. Travel agents can be more demanding, so patience and competence become key virtues for the airline reservationist.

What are some of the attributes of an agent that are desired by the airline? A pleasing telephone voice and friendly personality that comes across through voice alone are chief attributes. The airline prefers someone with a knowledge of geography, which will enhance the agent's ability to make key connections for clients traveling to hard-to-reach destinations. An agent should have sharp mathematics skills, keen reasoning ability, and good judgment. The airline also would like someone who has experience with a computer or keyboard, as the agent will utilize the computer during the entire duty period. Airline computers differ from

the systems used in the general business world, so an agent must be trained to use the specific airline system. Travel schools usually offer some computer training, and the airlines themselves train reservation agents prior to their first contact with clients or travel agents. Top airline computer systems include American's SABRE, United's APOLLO, and TWA's PARS.

Working Conditions

The airline reservation sales agent usually works in a large central office answering customer questions by phone and booking customer reservations. The working conditions are typically pleasant, clean, and climate-controlled. The majority of agents enjoy each other's company as they encounter similar problems and amusing circumstances.

The problems associated with the agent's work are irregular hours, pressure of handling calls expeditiously, and trying to pacify the traveler under stressful conditions. Eyestrain and wrist problems from hours on the computer are occupational hazards.

Salary

Industrywide information on the salaries of reservation sales agents is not available. However, one may look at a major carrier and deduce some information. The data presented here are from a major carrier that did not wish to be identified. The figures are from June 1989. This particular carrier has an A-and-B pay scale, the levels of which reach parity in the sixth year of employment. A-scale salaries go to agents who have already worked for the company, while B-scale wages are paid to new hires. The B-scale agent receives $14,112 annually to start. If someone within the company, who was hired prior to June 1984, transfers up to this same job, that agent would make the A-scale wage of $19,596 to start. Employees on both A and B scales receive yearly increases in salary. In the fifth year, the last year before reaching parity, the A-scale agent makes $27,444 and the B-scale agent makes $19,764. Both agents make $28,752 during their sixth year. The pay scale for the tenth year is $35,316. Supervisors make 18 percent more than agents, which at the tenth year would average $41,672. Other positions, largely administrative or managerial, associated with this type of work are sales manager and regional director. Salaries are commensurate with the level of responsibility.

Employment Outlook

The need for reservation agents is rather constant. The employment of such agents depends upon turnover from such factors as retirement, burnout, firings, and the normal fluctuations of the industry during economic changes. To apply for a job, contact the airline for which you wish to work. A list of major airline corporate addresses appears in Appendix A. It is, of course, helpful if you live in or near the city where the reservations center is located. You may determine that by calling the airline for which you wish to be an agent.

The Bottom Line

Reservation agents can make an excellent income, after a few years of work with a company. While the work is fast-paced and sometimes stressful, successful agents learn to enjoy it. Full-time agents enjoy all the perks of airline employees, such as free or greatly discounted flight, pensions, benefitis, stock options, and insurance. Some airlines also employ part-time agents. Though such employees typically do not qualify for the perks, they are able to be a part of the industry while having more time for other activities outside of work. If you have that special personality which communicates well by voice alone, you may do well in the world of the reservation agent.

FLIGHT ATTENDANT

The flight attendant is the person who may be most responsible for the client's overall perception of the airline. The client never actually sees the reservation agent, who works by phone from a remote location. The client is in contact with the person who issues the boarding pass for only a few moments. The gate attendant is usually too busy to be involved with each client for very long. The pilots almost never come in direct contact with the client, except to say goodbye when the passenger deplanes. As the airline's most visible representative, the flight attendant is left to mold the company image.

The flight attendant was formerly referred to as a stewardess, as the career field until recently was almost totally dominated by women. This came about because the first flight attendants were nurses—members of another profession heavily populated by women. These attendants were aboard primarily to care for the apprehensive early air traveler. Early commercial flight was noisy, rarely climate-controlled, and not pressurized, which could cause nausea. Early airplanes frequently got caught in rough air, since they could not climb high enough to get above weather. A flight attendant/nurse could be very valuable.

Today flight conditions are smoother, and the nurse is no longer a necessity. However, a new breed of flight attendant is required. The passenger has come to expect more service during the flight. The flights are shorter in time, the number of passengers per flight is increasing, and competition among the airlines is stiffer. This certainly requires a flight attendant who knows what to do and can do it quickly, but who also has a friendly personality and relates well to others.

Education

The major airlines want to hire college graduates if at all possible. Practically all major carriers indicate in their employment literature that they prefer at least two years of college or two years of equivalent business experience. Some will accept other work experiences which involve considerable public contact in lieu of some college. The number of flight attendants with a college degree is increasing each year. This is not unique, as we see many career fields that once hired high school graduates now requiring a college degree for entry.

You can obtain a feel for the type of courses to take by reviewing a specific airline's requirements for a flight attendant. You may receive the requirements by writing or calling a particular airline of your choice. You will see such requirements as good English usage, effective conversational skills, and foreign language being desirable. The airline also looks for attributes that may not be learned in class, such as maturity, emotional stability, an outgoing personality, poise, ability to work under stress, and flexibility in terms of relocating.

The training of a flight attendant usually requires somewhere in the vicinity of six weeks. The majority of training is conducted by the hiring airline. The airline may pay the future attendant a modest salary and provide lodging and meals during the training as well as free transportation to the training site. Not everyone accepted for training will graduate from the program. Several people probably will remove themselves from training after discovering that the job was not what they had perceived it to be. Others will be dropped from training by the airline because they do not meet the requirements of the training program. One major airline indicated that usually more trainees remove themselves than the airline drops.

The training is developed around three major areas of concern: 1) flight safety, 2) customer service, and 3) marketing. The passenger is rarely aware of the tremendous amount of safety training required of the flight attendant. The FAA lists very specific functions that each attendant must be able to perform, along with certain regulations that each attendant must know. The FAA also requires recurrent training each year on safety factors related to the type of aircraft to which the attendant is assigned. Most airlines exceed the FAA requirements in training attendants on safety measures. Attendants will be aware of emergency exits, methods of getting out of the aircraft, and how to be ready for unique events like ditching over water. The rigorous training may include simulation of emergency situations, such as trying to find exits and remove passengers in a plane filled with dense smoke. Flight attendants also will be proficient in cardiopulmonary resuscitation (CPR) and in emergency measures for heart attacks, extracting food lodged in someone's throat, and a dozen other emergency procedures.

The airline and the FAA hope that no attendant will ever have to utilize emergency procedures, but reality suggests that many will. There are numerous and recent accounts of heroic measures taken by attendants both on board and during a crash. Attendants have delivered babies, maintained CPR on heart attack victims, calmed hijackers and terrorists who had taken over a plane, moved through the aircraft ministering to numerous passengers when half the plane's roof had ripped off, and performed other unusual activities for which their training prepared them. Some were capable of rising to the unexpected for which no training can prepare.

Another element of training, and the one more frequently encountered on the job, is the everyday duty of welcoming passengers aboard, serving them food and drinks, and wishing them a good flight. This element takes up a considerable period of training time, for it is the routine in which the attendant will spend the majority of the working flight. It also involves the third element of training—marketing—which sells company services and is becoming an increasingly important part of the flight attendant's job description.

Working Conditions

Some of the job functions of the flight attendant were covered in the section on training. When a new flight originates at a particular airport, the flight attendant crew will have arrived several minutes prior to the scheduled flight. The attendants will meet with the captain, who will brief them on the flight. Such items as weather, passenger load, expected delays, and any other unique features of the flight are discussed. Sometimes only the senior attendant meets with the captain and will then pass information on to the other attendants. The attendants will then go aboard the airplane and check on conditions such as food and drink supplies, whether the cleaning crew was thorough, if everything is in place as it should be, and whether the proper forms and safety equipment are aboard.

One or more of the attendants will stand at the gate to take tickets or look at the boarding passes of oncoming passengers. Another attendant will be just inside the cabin door greeting passengers and assisting those who need extra help. Particular attention is paid to small children, children traveling without parents, handicapped persons, and clients who are flying first class. The major chore is to get everyone seated, make sure their carryons are properly stowed, and see that conditions conform to FAA requirements.

As the aircraft begins to taxi, one attendant will read or recite the safety information required by the FAA. Such information relates to smoking restrictions, placing seat backs and tray tables in the upright position, having safety belts fastened, and making sure carryons are placed under the seat or in the closed overhead bins. As this attendant is talking, the other attendants are stationed throughout the airplane, demonstrating the safety measures to the passengers. When the announcement is completed, all attendants will move throughout the cabin to confirm that their directions were followed. The captain will announce to the attendants to be seated for takeoff or will sound a gong that will alert the attendants.

As soon as the airplane has reached cruising altitude, the attendants will begin to see to passenger needs. They may serve a snack or a full meal, hand out reading material, or provide pillows and blankets if the trip is an extended one. Headsets are quite popular for extended flights, where a movie may be screened. Some flights have video games that may be rented and telephones with which passengers may call people on the ground. The future is already here aboard several aircraft, which are equipped with video screens in the seat backs. Up to four channels may be selected on these sets. First-class passengers may be served a seven-course meal on international flights, including champaign and many different wines. The attendant must be well-versed in the niceties of life to compete in today's market.

Upon arrival at the designated airport, the attendants will again assure that safety precautions are on the minds of all passengers. After the passengers have deplaned, the attendants may straighten up for the next group or may fill out numerous forms required by the airline and the FAA. Or they may, like some passengers, hurry to catch the next flight. It is not uncommon for both flight crew and flight attendants to change planes in the hub airports, just as passengers do.

Attendants typically work 65 to 85 flying hours per month. They may have up to 80 hours of nonflight duty time per month as well. Some of this may involve additional training, layover time, and paperwork. Supervisors will have additional duties. Flight time and duty hours are determined by FAA regulations and the contract that is negotiated between the flight attendants' union and the airline management. The majority of attendants are union members. Contracts are normally negotiated for a period of three years. Some unionized attendants have had to go on strike to obtain the benefits they desire. Most union strikes have met with disaster in recent years, however.

Flight assignment is usually based on seniority. The attendants "bid their flights"—that is, list their preferences, in the same manner as do the pilots. Normally the longer the attendant has been with the airline, the better the opportunity for being assigned to desired flights. New attendants may have to wait several years before being assigned to the more sought-after international flights. There are some exceptions to this. The need for attendants who are fluent in languages other than English may allow a new graduate who speaks a second language to be assigned to international flights. Such flights pay more and afford a greater number of days off than do domestic flights. The normal domestic flight scenario is two days flying and three days off. The international flight is two flying and five off. An attendant can make as few as three international flights per month for a full month's pay.

Flight attendants who have seniority can allow their flights, which are usually the more desirable flights, to pass to someone else and simply take time off. This gives flexibility to the life-style of the attendant. She or he may wish to do somethinge else for a while, like travel, write, go to school, or stay at home with a new baby. Whatever the reason, it can be arranged. Some airlines will release an attendant for up to a year to complete college and may offer additional financial incentives to do so. Some airlines will even allows attendants to be part-time employees, working perhaps only one or two flights per month.

Salary

Flight attendants receive a rather good salary for the time they put into their work. However, one should understand that no salary adequately compensates a person who may face the danger that can confront the attendant in case of disaster in the air. Flying is generally safe. No other form of transportation approaches the safety record of the airlines. But at 30,000 feet, traveling at 500 miles per hour, anything can happen.

The airlines vary in what they pay attendants. There cannot be too great a discrepancy between the same class of carrier. That is, major airlines tend to pay similar wages. National airlines have a competitive wage structure, and other levels of carrier will be similar. One recent development in the salary of attendants is referred to as A-scale and B-scale. New attendants are hired at a lower salary than the more senior attendants. They may reach parity at some point. However, the time period may vary for up to nine years. Such pay scales are also a matter of union negotiation. Some feel that such a pay scale conspires to cause a rift between A- and B-scale attendants, making for a strained working climate.

According to the Future Aviation Professionals of America (FAPA), which offers a flight attendant employment referral service, the average beginning base salary for an attendant with a major airline is $12,324 per year. The fifth-year attendant averages $21,264 maximum. The senior attendant can earn up to $33,768 on average. Obviously, some airlines pay above the average, some below.

Another factor which must be considered is that attendants are paid a per-hour rate for expenses when on duty. The average for major carriers is $1.42 per hour. Airlines with international routes usually pay more per hour to attendants on those routes. An attendant can earn up to an additional $480 per month—tax free—which comes to $5,760 per year. That can be significant.

The average beginning salary for attendants with national carriers is $12,072 per year. The fifth-year maximum salary averages $19,848. The maximum senior attendant salary averages $27,732. Hourly expense pay averages $1.29. Large regionals, or what FAPA calls 'turbojet airlines,' average $11,592 to start, and smaller regionals average $10,740 to begin.

Employment Outlook

The employment outlook for flight attendants seems very good throughout the 1990s. In fact, except in really poor economic times, when everyone is affected, flight attendants have a good prospect for employment. There has been an increase in routes and the number of aircraft operated by airlines since deregulation of the industry in 1978. There isn't a considerable turnover of attendants, though burnout claims some. Early retirement certainly affects the industry, as older attendants tend to desire more stability of family and geography.

One change that has come about in recent years, however, is that many flight attendants are flying for a greater number of years. Years ago, a stewardess could be fired if she gained weight, got married, or simply became "too old," the standards being arbitrarily decided by the employer. The airlines wanted young, single, attractive women as a lure for male business travelers. Today, because of antidiscrimination legislation, a flight attendant may be female or male, single or married, with or without children, and of any race or ethnic origin. Height and weight restrictions have been eased, and the attendant may fly as long as she or he is physically fit, or until age 70. Some carriers are even hiring flight attendants who are presently 50 years of age and older.

More than 20,000 attendants were hired in 1989 by U.S. airlines. The major airlines hired the greatest number of attendants. According to FAPA, 72 percent of the new hires went to the majors. The majors employ over 87 percent of all attendants with U.S. carriers. The national airlines employ nearly 9 percent of the attendant work force. FAPA estimates that some 100,000 attendants will be hired during the 1990s, or approximately 10,000 per year. The majority of these will be hired by the major carriers. The major domiciles and the larger bases will be where the greatest number of attendants will be based. Some airlines allow their attendants to commute—that is, to live at a distant place and catch nonworking flights to their assigned base. Most airlines do not allow reserve attendants to commute. You may have to move to the assigned base city until you have enough seniority to get off reserve. Some bases are 'very senior,' and you could be on reserve for years.

The Bottom Line

Being a flight attendant can be exciting. It can allow you to meet new people, sometimes very important people. You certainly get to travel. You also have excellent travel benefits during your free time, which will allow you to see the world at very little expense. With several airlines, your family receives some free travel and additional discounted travel. The pay is good for the time worked. There are other liberal benefits such as stock options, bonuses when the airline is doing well financially, insurance programs, and retirement. Disadvantages of a career as a flight attendant include erratic schedules that may conflict with family activities, physical wear and tear—on the feet especially, problems with unpleasant passengers, and the slim possibility of an accident aboard the plane. But most flight attendants believe that the enormous benefits far outweigh these drawbacks. Being a flight attendant is something you could really get up in the air about!

AVIONICS TECHNICIAN

There was a time in the aviation industry when the avionics technician was basically an airframe or power plant technician with some additional knowledge or experience with radios. Radios were used primarily for communication. That era has long since passed. The avionics technician is a specialist in electronics and may even further specialize in particular systems of communication and navigation.

The crowded sky is kept safe, to a large degree, by the electronic devices installed in the airplanes which allow communication through similar devices on the ground. The air traffic controller of a bygone era maintained aircraft separation principally by talking with the pilots and interpreting information given by those pilots. Today the radar screen contains a blip representing the airplane, but also its flight number, the altitude at which it is flying, its direction, and its speed. In the very near future, the airplane will have equipment on board that will monitor other aircraft in the vicinity. It will even alert the pilot of an impending collision and suggest what action to take. The FAA intends to develop a system that will make verbal communication between the pilot and the air traffic controller almost obsolete. One can readily see the extent to which the avionics technician of the future must be trained.

Education

The avionics technician may receive formal education in a variety of ways. The airline industry would prefer that one have the airframe and power plant (A&P) certification, along with the appropriate Federal Communications Commission (FCC) license. There is reason to believe that the impending shortage of avionics technicians will cause a major separation of avionics from the

A&P, such that the majority of technicians will not likely have education in both. The educational process is becoming too complex and protracted to appropriately educate for such a broadly experienced person.

Avionics technicians are educated at all levels and in all types of schools, just as is the A&P technician. Colleges, universities, junior colleges, technical schools, a few high schools, and a large representation of *proprietary* (profit-making) schools educate the majority of avionics personnel. The military also contributes to such training. A typical program of training will last from 14 months to 24 months. The majority will be between 18 and 24 months in length.

Basic electronics is essential to a thorough understanding of avionics. The potential technician should like aviation, be competent in mathematiucs, and be capable of communicating effectively. There is a greater possibility of a person doing well in avionics if the person understands the avaiation environment. It is one thing to understand a principle that works on a test bench, but it is altogether different in real life to realize the stress of going from sea level to 40,000 feet several times per day, as airplanes do.

Certification

The certification of avionics technicians is different from that of A&P technicians. One difference is that the avionics technician's license comes not from the FAA, but from the FCC. There are several levels of licensing related to the different types of equipment serviced and what the technician is allowed to do to the equipment. For example, the avionics technician does not install or remove avionics equipment from the aircraft unless the technician also has an A&P certificate. What the avionics technician does to the equipment depends upon the level of FCC license held.

Working Conditions

The environment in which the avionics technician works is friendlier, at least weatherwise, than that of the A&P. Most avionics work is accomplished indoors "on the bench"—that is, inside an avionics laboratory. Some outside work may be required in the nose cone of the aircraft, which contains the radar equipment. Avionics equipment is normally quite clean and free of oil and grease, thus the avionics technician has a more hygienic environment in which to work. The equipment is normally enclosed and in modules that are easy to handle.

Salary

The avionics technician often is paid at a slightly higher rate than the A&P who is not also licensed in avionics. With the major carriers, the average beginning hourly rate is $13.81, compared to $13.57 for the A&P, according to the Future Aviation Professionals of America (FAPA). The greater difference seems to exist at the foreman level. For example, the average salary for the major airline foreman in avionics is almost $6,000 per year greater than the foreman with only the A&P. The difference is even greater for the foreman and the line worker who are employed by the national and regional airlines, although the beginning and maximum salaries are lower than those with the major carrier.

Employment Outlook

The forecast for the avionics technician for the next several years is excellent. Because of the increased electronics use in modern aircraft, it is impossible for the A&P to keep up with the technology. The greatest need of the airlines at present is for bench-test qualified avionics personnel. These technicians actually disassemble the units and determine where the problems exist. One major carrier, however, requires that all A&P technicians hired have 750 hours of electronics/avionics experience, or appropriate schooling in lieu of experience.

Information from the industry tends to indicate that practically all graduates of avionics schools are offered jobs immediately. Refusing to relocate is about the only drawback to rapid employment in the avionics field. Graduates of one West Coast school receive, on the average, 12 job offers. Most schools indicate a placement rate in the 90-percent range. While the airlines seek experienced technicians, they will probably hire more workers directly from school as the crunch worsens. At present, general aviation and the larger avionics shops are the training grounds for most fresh graduates of avionics schools.

The Bottom Line

Avionics technicians are highly sought electronics specialists. Salaries range from the beginning average with major airlines of $13.81 per hour, or around $27,620 per year, to $48,940 per year for supervisors. The job outlook is superb. The working conditions are usually among the most desirable. Avionics technicians work in a variety of jobs not associated with airlines, which will be discussed in upcoming chapters. If you like mathematics and you can communicate well, avionics could provide an "electrifying" career!

OTHER AIRLINE POSITIONS

The airlines hire people with a diversity of expertise, education, and professional ability. Aside from the jobs already described in this chapter, there are far too many airline positions to list and define them all. One airlines lists and briefly describes more than 220 positions—and lists an additional 230 positions that are not described. That comes to over 450 titled positions with a single major carrier. Several of the positions have to do with the same major area of expertise but list different responsibilities within that field. An example would be that of an analyst. There are 46 positions listed for this one skill. It is obvious that most analysts do similar things. In this case, they do it for different departments, thus creating 46 different job classifications.

If you have a particular skill or some special knowledge, contact the airlines of your choice and find out whether they can use you in their lineup.

CHAPTER 3

AIRPORTS

There are more than 16,000 airports in the United States. An airport can be a grass strip located on a farm in Montana or an immense complex of concrete, metal, and people located in a major city. Fewer than 700 of our airports have scheduled air carrier service. The smaller airports are served by general aviation airplanes. Approximately 5,000 airports have a paved runway. Varying sizes and uses of airports require that those who operate them be of equal diversity.

A small airport may be operated by one person or may be a family operation, affectionately referred to as a ''mom-and-pop'' operation. This type of airport is a dying breed for several reasons. The technology required for maintenance, flight training, charter, and other airport operations is changing so rapidly that Mom and Pop can no longer keep up. Many of the smaller operations are also being edged out by residential encroachment. Many airports across the nation close every year. FAA regulations are changing markedly, requiring safety fencing, costly environmental controls on storing fuel, and the ever-increasing paperwork, which leaves little time for other things that must be accomplished.

The large airports may require thousands of employees to maintain a daily operation. The large airport is frequently compared to a large city. It has its own police force, fire department, maintenance crew, managers, stores, transportation system, parking lots, restaurants, even banks and places where businesspeople can obtain typing services, photocopies, and FAX capability. An operation of this magnitude must have some very specialized workers. Let's consider a few of them.

AIRPORT MANAGER

The airport manager of a medium sized airport must be experienced in several areas such as business management, civil engineering, personnel management, public relations, finance and of course, aviation. The very large airports will provide for a staff wherein the special expertise is available through several assistants to the manager.

Education

The airport manager of just a few years ago probably came to the job in one of several ways: military service, which involved operating airfields; experience in directing a large fixed base operation (FBO), a self-contained unit that provides a variety of services and usually is located on a medium-to-large airport; political appointment; or by working as an assistant to the manager of a medium-to-large airport.

Today an increasing number of airport managers are coming from colleges and universities that have programs specifically for educating the airport manager. Such courses of study are often found in the college's school of basic and applied sciences. The emphasis is on science, mathematics, computer science, and aviation management, with selective business courses in finance, human resource management, accounting, and marketing. It never hurts to have an additional course or two in psychology and public speaking.

The manager must defend budgets and expansion plans before the airport board. It is not uncommon for the manager to speak before civic clubs, visiting airport contingents, public forums concerned with noise from the airport, and other interested groups.

Certification

There is a special and very exclusive certification available for the airport manager who is skilled, experienced, and will go through a rather long and very specific program of education. This program is available from the American Association of Airport Executives and allows a graduate to place the initials AAE after his or her name, much in the same manner as one who holds the doctorate. The certification is actually called accreditation and requires that the candidate have at least three years of airport management experience, write an original paper on some phase of airport management, and pass oral and written examinatiions on a level comparable to other professions. A four-year college degree, or its equivalent, is required. There are fewer than 300 accredited airport executives in the United States.

Working Conditions

The airport mamanger is almost daily involved in enforcing airport and FAA rules and regulations, planning and supervising maintenance, and designing safety and security programs. The manager also is concerned with negotiating leases with airport tenants and airlines, programming future needs, developing budgets, promoting the use of the airport, training and supervising employees, and increasingly dealing with irate groups who are concerned with the noise from airports. It is a busy life and rarely dull.

Being an airport manager at medium and large airports is not an entry-level position. A person usually rises to this level by managing smaller airports or by working in the operations division of larger airports. One way to enter the operations department at many airports is through an internship while attending college. Numerous colleges, especially those with aviation programs, interact with airports to place students while they are in school. Some colleges have cooperative education programs with airports hundreds of miles from the campus. Students placed in these positions will live in the city where the airport is located for up to three alternating semesters, working full-time at the airport.

The size of the airport and the specific title of the person will largely dictate whether he or she spends the majority of time indoors or outside. The young operations worker spends considerable time outside driving around runways and taxiways, perimeter fences, and other areas, checking on the condition of the airport. FAA regulations require periodic checks on areas where planes are operating. Weather changes require the operations specialist to frequently check on runway conditions. Summer weather requires more frequent review of maintenance crews who cut grass and maintain the landscape. As experience is gained and more responsibility is assumed, the operations worker will tend to concentrate more time indoors.

Due to the fact that less than 10 percent of all airports are privately owned, a job in airport management is a job in public administration. Once an entrepreneur, probably with flight experience, the airport manager today is skilled in the governmental process and the business management of a public institution. Such an administrator will be first of all a professional, will be good at problem solving, and will be politically sensitive.

Salary

Salaries of airport executives, like most salaries, will vary with education, experience, and other qualifications, as well as with the size and complexity of the hiring airport. More airports are exploring the hiring of what they call interns, for periods of time normally in the vicinity of 18 months. These internships differ from the normal definition of an internship in that these positions are full-time paid positions for college graduates. The usual internship is a part-time position for students who are attending college. The full-time intern is paid from $15,000 to $18,000 per year to start.

Salaries for experienced managers who have a college degree will range from $28,000 to over $40,000 annually. Executives at major airports may be paid more than $100,000. Progressive experience is important to the hiring airport. Two to five years in an operations department, movement to deputy or assistant manager, and finally promotion to airport manager is the normal route to higher salaries. Air carrier-type airports prefer to hire lower-level managers who have experience at air carrier airports. The larger airports tend to advertise for the accredited airport manager. Such accreditation usually will command a higher salary. Many airport employees, due to the public nature of airports, will have fixed salaries, or a salary range that is dictated by specific years of previous related service. Such salaries rarely are open to negotiation.

Employment Outlook

Due to the operating complexity of airports in today's environment, the job outlook for well-trained managers is positive. The majority of positions will obviously occur in states having the largest number of attended airports. States such as California,

Texas, Florida, Illinois, New York, and Pennsylvania will have the greater number. Entry-level positions will occur in larger numbers at airports served by air carriers. The National Association of State Aviation Officials (NASAO) indicates that a critical need exists for college-educated airport planners and engineers. One may sometimes have to accept underemployment to break into airport management. The author knows one former student who spent a summer cutting grass at an airport in order to show his desire. He is now the operations director for that hub airport and has numerous subordinates reporting to him.

Airports contribute billions of dollars to the economy of the nation. Even community airports can be a valuable asset to the local economy. A medium-sized airport in western Tennessee contributes over $1.7 billion to the state economy in terms of wages, sales, taxes paid, and purchases made. Such airports operate around-the-clock, seven days a week, and on holidays. Operations personnel, unlike some other airport workers, must be represented around-the-clock.

The Bottom Line

Airport management can provide a satisfying career, especially if you like working with people. The career provides a variety of experiences, with rarely a dull moment. Increasing complexity requires much more education than in previous years. With the tremendous growth in air carrier service since 1978, airports have become greatly congested on both the air side and the land side. Innovative managers are needed to help solve the increasing problems. The pay is not as great as a comparably responsible position in the corporate world, but the excitement and the opportunity to be your own boss, to a certain degree, may compensate for lower salaries.

OTHER AIRPORT CAREERS

You can see that the airport is often as diverse as a medium-sized city. As such, a variety of careers are available to accommodate almost every level of education and professional expertise. The airport needs workers in the major categories of craft trades, including electricians, plumbers, and carpenters. People with backgrounds in accounting, finance, personnel relations, and civil engineering also are needed. In addition, emergency services personnel such as firefighters, police officers, and paramedics are required. Finally, maintenance workers, skycaps, clerks, restaurant workers, and concessionaire employees can find airport jobs. Some of these workers are employed directly by outside contractors instead of by the airport. However, the airport personnel office can advise you of jobs in that category.

FIXED BASE OPERATOR

Commonly referred to as an FBO, a fixed base operator fulfills a business function that is absolutely required for general aviation to survive. However, FBOs exist on all airports, not just general aviation airports. Thus, it is appropriate that we place the section on the FBO in the chapter on airports.

The typical FBO provides fuel, maintenance, flight instruction, and coffee. (Coffee is listed a bit tongue-in-cheek; however, coffee sometimes becomes as important as fuel to the pilot and passengers!) An FBO may also provide charter and air taxi services, crop dusting, aerial advertising, airplane rental, aircraft sales, and hangar rental. Some FBOs provide baggage delivery service for airlines. This involves baggage that does not arrive with the passenger and must be forwarded to the owner. One can readily see the job possibilities with FBOs.

The FBO may be a mom-and-pop operation at a small airfield, or it may be a large, multimillion-dollar operation utilizing the expert services of dozens of people. Several of the larger FBOs have established operations at numerous airports across the nation. Such companies often purchase an operating FBO and convert it to the name and operational directives of their other places. General aviation pilots become familiar with the services of these companies and tend to utilize them wherever they fly. Many FBOs also service major carrier airlines and commuter operations.

The Federal Aviation Administration (FAA) regulates practically every function of aviation. Each service provided by the FBO is regulated under one or more sections of the Federal Aviation Regulations. A person might create a position with an FBO simply by understanding the various regulations and being able to file the appropriate forms on behalf of the FBO. The future looks as though we may become more, rather than less, regulated. The FBO may also have to conform to requirements of the airport at which it does business. Some airport authorities require that the FBO provide certain services in order to operate. Typical offerings are flight instruction, fuel, maintenance, and aircraft storage.

Education

FBOs vary so much in size and personnel that it is difficult to discuss their employment needs. In the past, many young people started a career in aviation by working for an FBO in exchange for flight time. Those days are almost gone, due in large part to federal regulations concerned with minimum wages, child labor laws, and all of the restrictions regarding such factors as social security, income tax deductions, and hazardous working conditions. An occasional FBO may still be willing to hire workers without a specialty or skill to do odd jobs like cleanup, fueling, and washing aircraft. The educational level for such workers may be less than high school However, that is becoming rare as well.

Today the typical FBO will hire maintenance technicians, pilot/instructors, secretaries, marketing personnel, and—depending upon the size of the operation—dispatchers and charter pilots. The educational level of such workers will vary from one FBO to another. Some may be college-educated. Others may have specialized schooling beyond high school that does not include a college degree.

Certification

Certification applies to the pilots and maintenance technicians. Special qualifications may also apply to the chief pilot and dispatchers. The FAA regulates all such certification.

Working Conditions

Working conditions vary from one FBO to another. Several of the "chain" FBOs have multimillion-dollar physical plants. Million Air has recently opened the 27th FBO in its network. Beech Holdings owns 18 FBOs and is the parent company of the Beech Aircraft Company. AMR Combs currently owns nine FBOs but will no doubt expand rapidly. AMR is the parent holding company of American Airlines. AMR intends to expand its charter operation into a national network, while at the same time increasing aircraft sales and service.

The type of FBO being opened today is light years away from the facilities of the past. Fort Lauderdale Jet Center opened in late 1989 and is somewhat typical of what we will see in the future. Its terminal covers 120,000 square feet and comes complete with pilot's lounge, sleeping room, sauna, gym, and showers. The center has three conference rooms, audio-visual equipment for meetings, rental cars, a gift shop, catering services, and a shuttle to the airline terminal. U.S. customs and agriculture inspection station is located next door. There are 12 acres of ramp space and 36,000 square feet of hangar space, with more in the planning stages.

Compare that description with the old FBO that consisted or maybe 10,000 square feet, in which planes were stored *and* worked on, with one dirty bathroom used by everyone. An attached lean-to formed a business office, containing a desk, the required clock inset into a wooden propeller, and a few greasy rags that the owner/mechanic left on frequent trips from the hangar. Though you see a very different future for most of the FBOs, the old-style FBO is not extinct. Many an airline captain, Lear jet pilot, and general aviation mechanic have great memories left over from the FBOs of yesteryear.

Your working conditions will be different than they may have been 10 years ago. The FBO of today has competition. The name of the game is consistent, fast, and courteous *service*. Many people may initially be attracted to a glittering facility with lots of extras. However, unless the service aspect is also available, they will not likely remain long. Repeat customers are a must, and service is what brings them back.

Salary

There is a long-standing joke about FBOs that begins with a question: Do you know how to make a small fortune in aviation? Yes, go into the FBO business with a *large* fortune. This may be nearer the truth than we would like to believe. Even on the airfield where only one FBO has a monopoly business, it is at risk due to a large number of events. The basic economy affects aviation to a greater degree than it does most businesses. It is sometimes difficult to find competent and hardworking employees, especially in light of the great need for mechanics and pilots. High fuel prices can hit at the wrong time. New aircraft sales, especially in the training market, have been almost nonexistent in recent years. Environmental regulation, as it relates to buried fuel tanks, is of major concern and is quite costly to the FBO. Insurance, employee benefits, rising salaries, and the equipment necessary to maintain the more complex aircraft all increase the FBO's expenses.

Thus, salaries offered by your local FBO may be quite different from those offered a few states away. Rates of pay for the various kinds of jobs found at FBOs are detailed in chapter 5, on general aviation.

Employment Outlook

All of civil aviation is currently on an upswing in the United States. More people are learning how to fly than during previous years. Some 80,300 persons began learning how to fly during 1988. That figure rose to 88,972 for 1989. More qualified pilots are being hired today than were hired each year in the previous decade. Government and civilian research agencies talk of impending shortages of maintenance and avionics technicians and pilots. We know that the nation as a whole is moving away from production and into service-oriented businesses, which the FBO is. The future FBO will need all kinds of expertise to maintain its complex structure.

The Bottom Line

The FBO is changing. Perhaps you can be part of that change. If you like working with people, being around airplanes, and being the best at what you do, the FBO provides such an opportunity. Thousands of airports nationwide have one or more fixed base operators. They need all kinds of motivated people to assist in the operation of their businesses. Many are increasing their base into large charter operations. Some are involved in maintaining and refurbishing fleets of executive jet aircraft. Others supply fuel to the major air carriers. Many repair both the most complex jet and the small, single-engine training airplane, virtually side-by-side. If you meet the personal criteria listed above, you certainly have a place with the FBO.

CHAPTER 4

ENGINEERING RESEARCH
AND DEVELOPMENT

Research and development (R&D) activities occur in three primary places: in universities, within the major industrial corporations, and within governmental agencies. R&D activities are considered separately for the reason that R&D *becomes* the workplace. There are also many similarities in education, job function, and the manner in which researchers come to their positions.

People involved in R&D activities come from many fields of learning. Primarily, however, the majority tend to come from either engineering, mathematics, or the sciences. Engineers apply the sciences in the work which they perform. Engineering has developed primarily within the past 200 years, with more than 100 specialized engineering branches today.

The aerospace industry conducts more R&D than nearly any other industry. R&D also is a major contributor to the economic health of the nation. Without it, the country remains static and thus falls behind other nations in technological progress. The United States has been the leader in air carrier aircraft development since the beginning of aviation. The nation also leads in space development for commercial purposes and has practically been the sole supplier of general aviation aircraft and components.

Some of this is changing, with the entry of Japan and Europe into the space market, with Airbus making considerable inroads into the air carrier market, and with the virtual disappearance of training aircraft from the American marketplace (although the manufacture of training aircraft has recently been revitalized, to a degree, by Piper Aircraft).

R&D SPECIALIST

Education

The education of an R&D specialist should begin early in life, certainly by the time he or she enters high school. Four years of mathematics, with advanced courses where possible, are almost required. You should take all of the science courses offered in high school, especially the physical science courses. Communication skills also are absolutely necessary. You should begin to become familiar with computer languages at an early stage of development. If courses such as logic and reasoning are available, enroll in them. Do lots of reading, especially critical analyses and biographies of famous scientists and innovators in all areas. One or more foreign languages can be useful.

College brings the real commitment to intensive study. The first year is normally one of meeting general studies requirements. The sophomore year can be one of further exploration among the sciences and engineering. You should select a particular science, or the discipline of engineering, for concentration by the end of the sophomore year. Electives may be chosen in other sciences outside the major. A double major of science and mathematics could be a good choice.

Graduate school is a must for the researcher. Further concentration in the major, deeper study into the elements of research, and anything that will assist you in independent thinking should be a part of the one to three years of graduate study. A master's degree normally may be obtained within a calendar year. The doctorate may be added within two additional years, with hard work and excellent planning.

Working Conditions

The majority of a researcher's work takes place in the laboratory. Of course, the laboratory may be somewhat different in aerospace than in other areas. The researcher may be working in huge wind tunnels, in engine test facilities that would dwarf some factories, or at test ranges where rockets and supersonic engines are given final approval.

Many researchers do work in the traditional laboratory environment of chemicals, test tubes, ovens, and weird-sounding paraphernalia. They design new composites for airfoils, engines for hypersonic flight, flame-resistant materials for the interior of airplanes, and weapons systems for jet fighters. More recent developments in R&D include microelectronics, superconductivity, and robotics.

Salary

There is a tremendous variation in salaries, even within the professional R&D ranks. The typical R&D aeronautical engineer's salary is close to 50 percent higher than the typical industrial engineer's salary, although the gap decreased from 1989 to 1990. Salary profiles are closely related to educational level, years of experience, and the discipline within R&D that you have chosen to pursue. Table 4.1 shows 1990 median salaries of R&D specialists by discipline.

Table 4.1 Median Salaries of R&D by Discipline

Discipline	Salary
Aeronautical engineer	$56,111
Biologist	46,315
Ceramist	53,250
Chemical engineer	52,931
Chemist	48,312
Electrical engineer	50,978
Geologist	51,250
Industrial engineer	46,500
Mathematician	49,999
Mechanical engineer	49,280
Metallurgist	51,928
Physicist	54,500

Research and Development Magazine, March, 1990

Salaries in R&D range from less than $15,000 to greater than $90,000 per year. Due to the late acceptance of women into R&D, their salaries tend to cluster closer to the lower end of the professional scale. A larger percentage of women scientists tend to be in the discipline of biology and work for a university. Biology is the lowest-paying of the 12 disciplines listed in Table 4.1. The university simply does not have the funds to compete with industry.

Educational level is a factor in the salary of most careers. Careers not affected by educational level tend to be those in fields with strong unionization or ones where *seniority*—length of service—determines salary and other benefits. Even within those careers, a higher educational level may assist you in initially being hired over less-educated workers.

Information from *Research & Development Magazine* indicates that the R&D scientist or engineer with a doctorate may expect career earnings of $1,825,000 greater than a colleague with a bachelor's degree. Holding a doctorate makes a lifetime difference of nearly $1 million over the master's degree. And if you do not obtain a degree at all? The person with the earned doctorate is estimated to have a career benefit in excess of $3 million, or nearly $86,000 per year, over the person in R&D who does not obtain any degree. Earning a degree is not for everyone. It doesn't make one less of a person not to have a degree. However, if you are capable of earning a degree, more especially a graduate degree, your career earning power is multiplied several times.

Employment Outlook

The Bureau of Labor Statistics (BLS) projects a good climate for new scientists and engineers. Companies hiring electrical engineers will need a whopping 48 percent more by the year 2000. That will put the electrical engineer work force at some 600,000. Slower but consistent gains will be seen by life scientists at 21 percent, by physical scientists at 13 percent, and by aeronautical and astronautical engineers at 11 percent. Many of these increases will be in R&D positions.

The aerospace industry is a labor-intensive industry that employs as many salaried workers as production workers. This is unusual among manufacturing companies. The aerospace industry employs somewhere in the vicinity of 20 percent of all scientists and engineers in the United States.

The Bottom Line

The area of research and development offers the opportunity to explore, innovate, create, and develop to the limits of your own capabilities. It affords a comfortable living, a pleasant working environment, and the opportunity to interact with other researchers to produce the finest aerospace products in the world. Its future looks bright. Perhaps R&D can provide you with a most rewarding career.

TECHNICAL CHANGE

Working within a highly technical area requires that you remain up-to-date. If you work for a company that falls behind, the industry can pass right by and make it obsolete. You must assume individual responsibility for keeping up in technical matters.

CHAPTER 5

GENERAL AVIATION

General Aviation (GA) is more a concept than a workplace. GA is defined as all of aviation except the military and the airlines, thus it encompasses a huge segment of American aviation. Recent statistics state there were slightly over 220,000 active GA aircraft in the United States. Of these 89 percent—about 196,000 air craft—were piston engine airplanes. Of the approximately 24,000 craft remaining, about 24 percent, or around 5,800 craft, were *turboprop* planes—that is, they have a jet engine geared to a propeller. Another 18 percent, or about 4,300 craft, were *turbojet* planes, sometimes called *pure jet* aircraft. Approximately 28 percent, or about 6,700 craft, were *rotorcraft*—aircraft, such as helicopters, that are supported in flight by rotating airfoils. That leaves 30 percent, around 7,200 airplanes, to fit into various other classifications that are too diverse to list. These numbers are more meaningful when compared to the approximately 4,000 U.S. airline aircraft currently operating.

There are more than 700,000 licensed pilots in the United States. Fewer than 100,000 hold the air transport certificate, which is required of most airline pilots. The number of student pilot "starts" (beginning pilots) was down for several years until 1988, when new starts showed an increase. Additional starts were anticipated with the reactivation of the GI Bill in October 1990. The federal government will pay 60 percent of up to $10,000 for a veteran of the U.S armed forces to acquire the certificates needed to be employed as a pilot. The applicant must have a private pilot certificate and, of course, must qualify as a veteran.

A further comparison of general aviation with the airlines shows that GA flies 1.4 billion miles a year more than the U.S. airlines. GA annually flies some 53 million more flights and over 26 million hours more than the airlines in a given year. GA serves all 16,253 airports in the United States, whereas the major airlines fly into only about 240 of them. Regional airline service is available at some 573 airports.

GA, then, is a major contributor to the national economy and to the local economy in communities where a general aviation airport is located. This chapter will further define GA, will describe many of its needs for skilled and professional workers, and will yield information as to how you can enter the exciting world of general aviation.

DIVISIONS OF GENERAL AVIATION

GA is made up of several distinct divisions. General aviation flying is divided as follows:

1. business flying
2. executive flying
3. commercial flying
4. personal flying
5. instructional flying

Business flying consists of aircraft personally flown in the conduct of business, but not for compensation or hire. For example, if a person sells heavy equipment and if that person flies around the state or region talking with construction companies, state and local highway departments, and other users of bulldozers and graders, that salesperson is engaged in business flying.

Executive flying occurs when companies transport their employees or goods by air and use professional pilots to operate their aircraft.

Commercial flying is divided into several segments such as air taxi, rental aircraft, aerial application, and others.

Personal flying is just what it seems. A person owns or rents an airplane for transportation, for the sheer fun of flying, or perhaps even to show the airplane in competition with others.

Instructional flying is the utilization of an airplane to teach others how to fly. This may be, as described by a friend, a one-airplane/one-person/one sick-sack operation, or it can be a large school with dozens of airplanes and instructors. General aviation instruction customarily falls in between these two extremes.

BUSINESS AIRCRAFT USE

There are few aviation related jobs in companies wherein an airplane is utilized by the owner for the conduct of that company's business. You may become an accountant or a salesperson or have some other skill, plus a private pilot's certificate, and fly as part of that business. The difference is that you are flying on behalf of the business, not flying for hire for that company. You may *not* fly for hire unless you have at least a commercial certificate and instrument rating.

There is a tremendous amount of business flying in the U.S. However, most such flying does not involve a flight department or the need for aviation-related personnel. Aircraft utilized in business flying are normally maintained by a fixed base operator (FBO) and do not require crewing. While some aircraft are sophisticated jets and turboprops, the majority are light, single-engine airplanes that carry four to six persons on flights of approximately four hours duration. The famous golfer Arnold Palmer would be an example of a business flyer with his own jet airplane and jet helicopter. He also operates an aviation-related business, in addition to flying himself to golf tournaments.

EXECUTIVE FLYING

One of the most interesting areas of general aviation is that of executive flight. While it accounts for only 11 percent of all GA flying, it affords one of the greatest opportunities for employment. Executive flight requires professional pilots, maintenance crews, and—depending upon the size of the operation—flight schedulers, flight attendants, and managers of the flight and maintenance operations.

Why Executive Aircraft?

There are those who feel that flying corporate executives by private jet or turboprop airplane is pampering them beyond reason, in addition to the high salaries often paid to such executives. Nothing could be further from the truth. There are several reasons for using executive aircraft. Chief among them are to obtain maxium utilization of the executive's time and to protect the executive from possible terrorist attack in certain parts of the world.

A recent study of an executive's time pointed out that the senior executive of a corporation is actually worth 5.72 times his or her actual hourly rate to the company. Middle management's multiplier is 3.76. Time wasted in airports waiting on an airliner, sitting on the runway waiting for 20 jets ahead of you to take off, and circling in holding patterns above an airport while waiting for better weather or clearance to land, is not productive time for the executive of a corporation. These are among the pitfalls of executive travel on airlines. Now consider how much better the executive's time can be spent aboard a corporate jet, in conference with others in the company while moving directly from the home airport to the destination airport at 520 miles per hour.

The most modern company jet has a computer, FAX machine, VCR/TV, secretarial workstation, and full *galley* (kitchen) on board. These are comforts, true, yet they all save the time of a busy decision maker, enhancing that executive's worth to the company. Corporate jets can carry from 5 to 13 persons, depending upon the type of plane. There are other factors which are also important to the executive. Mental alertness and increased physical stamina of the executive, as compared to fatigue from flying the airlines, reduction in overnight stays away from home, and an improved work environment enroute all are good reasons for using the executive aircraft.

You might expect that the United States would have the largest fleet of executive aircraft, and it does. Approximately 70 percent of the world's executive fleet belong to American corporations. This provides much greater job opportunities for you. However, it might be interesting to spend a few years in another country. If you become certified and experienced with corporate-type aircraft, this would offer you the opportunity to work on similar aircraft in other countries. This is a very good way to see the world without being in the military.

The two leading producers of executive jets are Cessna, with several models of the Citation, and Learjet, with an equal number of different models. Coming on strong are Gulfstream, with the absolute top-of-the-line jet, and Dassault-Breguet, which makes the Falcon jet in several models, a couple of them with three engines. Believe it or not, some multinational corporations operate airliner-type aircraft, and some wealthy individuals also own personal jets of the size and type that major carriers fly.

Job Outlook

Corporations provide an excellent opportunity for the professional pilot and the maintenance technician in particular. Other positions are possible, such as flight attendant, flight department managers, and maintenance technician assistant. However, flight attendant positions are often "'on-call'" positions with little stability. Managers often rise from pilot or maintenance positions and are rarely hired directly to manage an operation. Other positions are possible but will require persistence.

Finding a corporate position is often more difficult than with an airline or a fixed base operator. There is less turnover in the corporate field. One of the best ways to obtain a corporate position is by referral and by having experience on the type of aircraft being flown by the company for which you wish to work.

Many corporations have helicopters in addition to jet and turboprop airplanes. The corporate helicopter is taking on many of the characteristics of the plush corporate jet. Many models are heavily soundproofed and have leather seats, telephones, small bars, and fold-out tables for conducting work while enroute. Some executive helicopters sell for as much as $4 million. The helicopter market took a nosedive, so to speak, in the early 1980s, due to the energy crunch. Revival of the industry began in 1987 and has continued steadily since. The helicopter has the greatest opportunity for growth of any part of the transportation industry, assuming we can solve the major problems of high maintenance costs and the lack of public heliports in convenient locations. Plenty of future job openings may be expected at Petroleum Helicopters, Inc. Based in Lafayette, Louisiana, the firm operates approximately 415 helicopters.

Salary

Rates of pay in executive aviation vary by experience, certificates held, geographic region of the nation, and size and financial strength of the particular company. Other factors contribute to salary, though not as significantly as those listed above. The National Business Aircraft Association (NBAA) has provided salary information for the job categories that follow.

PILOT SALARIES

Salaries of general aviation pilots who transport executives are, in most cases, considerably lower than salaries for comparable positions with many airlines. Some corporations, however, will impose more stringent requirements for applicants than will major carrier airlines.

Not everyone wants to fly for the airlines. Many pilots enjoy taking the same passengers on the majority of their flights. They become aware of expectations, where they will be going on most flights, who maintains their airplane, what the peculiar characteristics are of the plane they fly regularly, and how financially stable the company is. There are perks in both arenas of flight—air carrier and GA.

Captains for corporations had a *median* (figure that separates the top half from the bottom half) salary in 1988 of $48,733. Depending upon the type of aircraft flown, the median salary ranged from $41,160 for single-engine airplanes to $58,000 for heavy jets. Median salaries were highest in the western Pacific region. Pharmaceutical companies paid a slightly higher average salary than other types of companies.

Copilots received a median salary in 1988 of $35,000 per year. Median salaries ranged from $35,568 for single-engine planes to $41,500 for heavy jets. Once again, companies in the western Pacific region offered the highest salaries. The telecommunications industry paid copilots slightly higher salaries than other industries.

AVIATION DEPARTMENT MANAGERS

Managers of aviation departments are often senior captains who have stopped flying on a regular basis, or pilots who are still active and who assume managerial duties along with flying. The median base salary for managers in 1988 was $65,825. The East had the highest average salaries among the various regions. Pharmaceutical companies again led the industry in highest average salaries for this category.

The aviation department manager is something of a new breed of pilot in today's complex GA environment. The manager must have leadership qualities, normally vast experience as a pilot, ability to compare the several models of aircraft within the category the company can afford, computer literacy, financial responsibility, and capability to meet the demands of ''super'' executives within a highly competitive atmosphere. In short, the manager must have many of the same qualities that the senior officers of the corporations have.

CHIEF PILOT

Another category of quasi-manager/pilot which exists in executive aviation today is the chief pilot. This person may, in some smaller companies, also be the aviation department manager and the senior pilot. Job responsibilities that tend to define this person's position differently from that of the department manager have to do mainly with training. The chief pilot plans and implements the pilot training program of other company pilots, acts as the manager in the absence of the department manager, and may select and terminate pilots. The chief pilot may maintain the files of pilot currency and medical examinations as well as interacting with the FAA on pilot proficiency checks. The chief pilot may, in the absence of a company chief of maintenance, also be responsible for coordinating the maintenance technicians.

The chief pilot, of which there were nearly 700 responding to the 1988 NBAA survey, had a median annual base salary of $52,000. The range varied from those whose principal aircraft was a light twin-engine plane, at a median salary of $30,840, to the heavy-jet chief pilot with a median salary of $70,000. The western Pacific region was slightly ahead of the other regions, and the chemical industry tended to award higher salaries to chief pilots.

OTHER AVIATION-RELATED POSITIONS

Other workers found in executive aviation departments were flight attendants, with a median annual base salary of $27,067; chief of maintenance, $45,000; the A&P technician, $33,780; the maintenance technician helper, $21,960; and the scheduler/dispatcher, $24,900. Flight engineers, sometimes known as the third pilot, commanded a salary of $41,000. Flight engineers are found almost exclusively in companies with heavy jet aircraft.

Keep in mind that there is considerable difference among salaries paid in relationship to the size of the company, the type of aircraft on which pilots and technicians are qualified, the location of the company, whether the company flies international routes, and the business in which the company is engaged. The size of the department, the number of aircraft flown, the years of experience of the individual, and the income of the company also affect salaries. The best time to conduct research on the company for which you wish to work is while you are training for the type of position you want to perform. The more you know about that company, or the region in which you wish to be employed, the more likely you are to be hired.

While salary is important, it it by no means the *only* item to consider. You must be happy where you are working. You must have a philosophy that is in keeping with the type of company for which you wish to work. You will not be happy working for a chemical or petroleum company if you are a dedicated environmentalist. You might think ahead about raising a family and the type of environment in which you wish that to take place. Planning can rarely be overdone. You can always take advantage of serendipity should the opportunity arise.

Some of the perks of flying executive aircraft have to do with the sophistication of the airplanes. Some of the heavy executive jets, like the Gulfstream IV, the Falcon 900, and the Canadair Challenger, sell for up to $23 million. They have every state-of-the-art navigation device known. The more recent models have the "glass cockpit," a series of cathode ray tubes (CRTs) that display computer-generated symbols and information. The glass cockpit is replacing the rapidly disappearing engine and navigation instruments of older aircraft. The computers may be programmed to actually fly the airplane and keep the pilots advised of problems. Much of the maintenance is monitored by computers. The airplanes have speeds approaching Mach 1 (650 miles per hour at sea level), with most of the comforts of home.

Additional perks come in the form of international travel, vacations at resorts owned by the corporation, and the opportunity to meet captains of industry as well as public figures and celebrities who may have occasion to travel aboard company jets. Life within the corporate structure may be just what you seek.

COMMERCIAL AVIATION

Commercial aviation is difficult to define, in the sense that it encompasses such a wide variety of activities. Some of the flying is that which may be provided by a fixed base operator (FBO), as described in Chapter 3. Some of it falls into a category called charter and air taxi, which is often confused in terminology with small regional air carriers. Much of commercial aviation involves activities that are little-known to the general public. This section will briefly describe some of the activities of commercial aviation but will not delve into the salaries and working conditions. You can get a general feel for these factors by reviewing the sections in Chapter 3 concerning pilots and technicians.

Commercial aviation is made up of three divisions:

1. Air taxi/charter operations
2. Rental use
3. Aerial application and other uses

Air taxi operations involve any air carrier certified by the FAA that carries passengers for hire and meets specified minimum equipment regulations for flying in marginal weather conditions. The normal air taxi will operate over rather limited geographic areas, often within state boundaries.

Charter operators may function locally or may range all over the United States. These operators are normally certified under FAA Regulation Part 135, and they fly everything from nuts and bolts, to bodies, passengers, and bank checks. The general public is not aware of the many night activities of flying checks around this nation. Millions of dollars worth of checks wend their way by car or truck to a nearby local airport, are placed into a light, single-engine airplane, then are flown to a larger central airport to meet other planes. The checks are then loaded into a larger and faster jet to be flown to a location where up to a dozen or more jets will congregate, exchange checks, and do a reverse of the earlier operation. Such activity not only means great amounts of money to the banking industry, but it also provides numerous jobs for the aviation industry.

Rental use involves airplanes of all types, from the smallest trainer to large, multiengine turboprops. The majority of rental aircraft are those utilized in flight training. However, there are many qualified pilots who do not choose to own an airplane and who must rent an airplane for whatever purpose they choose to fly. Additional information on rentals may be found under the sections on FBOs in Chapter 3 and flight instruction later in this chapter.

Aerial application and other commercial uses. Aerial application is often called *crop dusting,* a reference to aerial spraying of pesticides over farm crops. It involves much more. Greater use of the airplane is being made for planting crops as well as controlling pests. Other commercial uses involve patrolling of pipelines and power lines, wildlife surveys, photography and aerial mapping, spotting for commercial fishing fleets, firefighting, and various police activities. The future of commercial aviation looks positive. It should grow with increased flexibility of aircraft development. Helicopters will come into wide and more popular use.

When considering your career in commercial aviation, you will begin by following one of the traditional routes to FAA certification, such as maintenance or pilot preparation, or by preparing yourself in an area that can be utilized within the aviation industry. Some colleges offer special programs that combine flight and agricultural expertise. Others offer independent departments of aviation and criminal justice, so that you can combine flight with law enforcement. A little research on your part will yield several combinations that can make you valuable to commercial aviation.

PERSONAL AVIATION

U.S. pilots logged more than 10 million hours of personal flying—that is, flying for pleasure—in 1986. Such flying can range from a couple of hours with the family on a Sunday afternoon to one of the more than 500 yearly flights by light aircraft across the Atlantic Ocean. Personal flying may take place in a 100-horsepower, single-engine, fixed-gear, *two-place* (two-seat) aircraft, or it may be in a Korean War vintage F-86 Supersabre fighter at speeds approaching 600 miles per hour. Whatever the reason, or the type of aircraft used, personal flying can be satisfying and beneficial. If you are interested in flying, but choose not to make a career of it, you may still wish to become a private pilot and own or rent an airplane for pleasure.

INSTRUCTIONAL FLYING

All pilot astronauts, fighter pilots for the armed forces, captains of major airlines, and aerobatic pilots at air shows began their flying at the same point—with zero experience. Not all went through the same type of training program. Not all flew the same type of aircraft in the beginning, and certainly each did not have the same motivation. Yet, they all began flying as we began life—at the "front end."

The front end for most pilots is a small-to-medium-sized airport, a two-place, single-engine airplane, and a young flight instructor with perhaps 300 to 900 hours of flight experience. For the military pilot-to-be, this may be somewhat different in that instruction may actually begin in a small jet, but the basics are still there. So when you stand in awe of the major airline captain who commands a giant Boeing 747, just remember, she or he got started in the same way you will have to begin.

Flight instruction is a means of "building time." Even with flight certificates and ratings abundantly available in your purse or billfold, you'd better have a minimum number of hours of actual flight time, or few employers will hire you as a pilot. One of the ways to obtain that all-important time is to instruct others in the art and science of flying. This not only helps to build time, but it also gives you some return on the investment of money already put into your own training.

A flight instructor may earn from $7 to $15 per hour for teaching in light aircraft. The instructor providing turboprop or other specialized instruction may earn even more. Some GA aircraft manufacturers hire pilots to teach their customers either how to fly or what they must know about the type of airplanes they sell. These are often salaried positions, and some pay very well.

There are professional flight instructors out there somewhere, but they are difficult to locate. They can stand to instruct only so many hours per day, due to the fatigue of teaching neophyte pilots. The airplane cockpit is not a good classroom, either. It is often noisy, filled with sunshine, tense due to surrounding traffic, and a containing student who may not know what is required next. The mental alertness required of the instructor can be overwhelming. The majority of instructors begin to burn out within a year or two and yearn for other types of flying. If you find a longtime professional from whom to take instruction, consider yourself a fortunate person indeed.

Flight instruction cannot take place without numerous other services being available. Fuel, hangars, maintenance, airport management, and related services are found where instruction is given. That means jobs for you, if you are interested in general aviation. Spend some time at an airport and observe what happens. You may find your niche in aviation there.

AIRPLANE SALES

Everyone is familiar with automobile dealerships and used car lots. The newspapers and television bombard us daily with advertising about the great deals we can get down at "Crazy Ernie's Car Emporium." However, you've probably never seen an ad for "Lucky Lindy's Plane Plaza!" Few of us realize the extent to which airplane sales are a major part of the aviation environment.

When you give it some thought, you realize that *someone* has to sell the hundreds of airplanes that are being manufactured each year. You now know that we are speaking of airplanes that may cost anywhere from $4,000 to $150 million and up. We will confine our comments primarily to general aviation aircraft. While the companies that build the F-16, the B-747, and the fast attack helicopter must also have sales representatives, these are rather specialized areas with limited job opportunities. Your best chance of being involved in airplane sales will come from general aviation.

Education

There are no specified levels of education required for a career in airplane sales. However, you need to be able to deal effectively with the kind of person with whom you come in contact. Will you be selling a small, two-place trainer to the blue-collar worker who always wanted to learn to fly and can now afford to do so? Or will you be showing a new Ag-Cat crop duster to a farmer? How about a $23-million Gulfstream IV to the owner of a major manufacturing company? What do you emphasize with each person? What kind of items do you believe will impress them? Your educational background can make a difference.

Working Conditions

Working conditions in airplane sales will vary considerably. There are two basic workplaces for the airplane sales representative. One is with the manufacturer, selling either from the factory or within the dealer organization in the field. The other is with a company that specializes in selling used aircraft. There will be some similarities. Both sales reps will be on the phone quite a lot, looking for prospects. The factory representative may receive more calls about the purchase of airplanes than the used aircraft counterpart. Some sales reps are constantly looking for used airplanes either to buy for resale or to list in their inventory of availability. There are several high-quality magazines and news sources that exclusively list airplanes for sale.

The factory representative accompanies airplanes to major trade shows like the National Business Aircraft Association (NBAA) meeting held each year. This show usually attracts about 14,000 people from around the world. This is "big sale" time. Some used aircraft companies also send aircraft to this type of show. The static display consists of dozens of airplanes worth untold millions of dollars.

Salary

You probably would assume that there is a difference between the person selling a small Cessna and one selling a Falcon 900. There is! A good salesperson can make a fine salary selling either. However, it stands to reason that the small-aircraft representative will have to sell quite a few more airplanes to make the same amount of money as the jet salesperson. In fact, the person selling the top-of-the-line jet likely will not sell more than five per year. The jet sales rep may earn an annual base salary from $30,000 to $50,000 or more, plus maybe $16,000 per plane in commission.

The total compensation is over $100,000 easily. Straight commission is the best deal, provided you are good at this business and can survive for a month or so without a sale.

Employment Outlook

The sales community is always looking for good sales representatives. You don't even have to possess a pilot's certificate, although it will enhance your opportunity for a job and for a sale if you do. You will probably have to start small and build your reputation. There are international opportunities as well as those in the United States. You also can find some good flight opportunities with the ferry companies that transport the airplane to the buyer. Some of those go to Australia and many to Europe. Any FBO that has a dealership may help you learn how to begin. Or ask at the FBO to see a copy of the advertising literature on airplane sales.

The Bottom Line

You first have to decide: do you want to sell, or fly, or make a lot of money? You may combine these, but you need to know your motivation. Airplane sales is a very competitive business, and you will feel like you are in a pressure cooker all the time. Some people thrive on such an atmosphere. Others burn out quickly. Your motivation will have some effect on which happens to you.

Learn as much as you can about airplanes. Know engines, avionics, performance standards. Learn relative prices. Know FAA directives and flaws about models that are "dogs." If you do your homework, you will receive the rewards.

OTHER GENERAL AVIATION FLYING

Each year, 5,000 aircraft and more than 900,000 hours of flight go into this category. It includes aircraft flown in support of aircraft sales, research, glider towing, and parachuting. Other uses are as diverse as you are innovative in thinking of ways to use aircraft. Further reading from books listed in the Appendix B bibliography will help you decide upon a career in general aviation.

CHAPTER 6

FEDERAL AND STATE GOVERNMENT

The federal government hires thousands of people to work in aviation-related positions. The Federal Aviation Administration (FAA) is the largest employer of civilians working in aviation within the federal employment system. Other positions are associated with such agencies as the National Aeronautics and Space Administration (NASA), the Civil Air Patrol (CAP)—a civilian auxiliary of the U.S. Air Force, the National Transportation Safety Board (NTSB), the U.S. Customs Service, and the Defense Mapping Agency.

Federal positions pay among the highest salaries, have an excellent retirement plan, normally involve working conditions that are pleasant, and provide excellent fringe benefits. Continuing education opportunities and generous vacation accumulation are among such benefits. The added advantage is that you also serve your country while earning a comfortable living.

FEDERAL AVIATION ADMINISTRATION (FAA)

The Federal Aviation Administration (FAA) is charged with the regulation of civil aviation in the United States. This involves the

certification of aircraft, pilots, maintenance technicians, maintenance and training facilities, and virtually everything pertaining
to aviation that requires approval. In addition to the above, the
FAA operates the airspace system, provides for aviation security,
and engages in engineering and development aspects associated
with planning the new airspace system. All of this adds up to an
awesome responsibility and requires the efforts of several thousand persons. The largest of the FAA's duties is to maintain the
air traffic control system.

The air traffic control (ATC) system consists of three related
facilities within which the air traffic controller works.

1. Flight Service Stations: provide pilot weather, emergency services, pilot advisories, and flight planning
   assistance. There are some 275 such stations within the
   U.S. and its territories. FSS, as they are known, are
   becoming automated, and positions will be gradually
   phased out.
2. Air Route Traffic Control Centers: control aircraft flight
   between airports and maintain safe separation of aircraft. There are 24 centers presently operating. Each
   center has responsibility for about 100,000 square miles
   of airspace.
3. Airport Control Towers: handle approach and departure
   aircraft as well as those which are moving on the ground
   at the airport facility. There are approximately 328
   airports with FAA control towers. The majority are
   operated by FAA controllers, though some are con-
   tracted to private companies.

The FAA employs more than 55,000 people. The diversity of
jobs within the FAA rivals that found within the airlines. The FAA
hires controllers, maintenance specialists, pilots, financial planners, engineers, analysts, managers, technical writers, public

relations personnel, human resource staff, and many other kinds of workers. Let's look at a few of these.

Air Traffic Controller

The ATC specialist controls aircraft and maintains safe separation of aircraft in the air and on the ground. The three types of facilities mentioned above will dictate to a great degree what the controller does, although the basic training is the same in the beginning. The successful controller talks with pilots, makes use of radar, has an excellent understanding of weather phenomena, recalls numbers well, and is able to communicate fluently.

EDUCATION

The applicant for ATC must have three years of work experience that demonstrate potential for learning and performing air traffic control work. Formal education may substitute for work experience. An excellent score on the aptitude examination, or having certain aviation certificates such as a private pilot or instrument rating, will also substitute for work experience. The ATC system is drawing significantly greater numbers of college graduates than in previous years. Perhaps the best way to qualify for ATC is to enter a college aviation program and enroll in the ATC cooperative education program. You will spend three extra semesters in college prior to graduating, but those semesters will be in full-time paid training at an ATC facility. This will prepare you for a most rigorous 11 weeks at the FAA Academy in Oklahoma City. The failure rate at the academy ranges between 40 and 60 percent. Without the several semesters of cooperative education experience, only the very best applicants survive the academy.

WORKING CONDITIONS

A controller works inside year-round. The tower controller rotates from a dark room filled with radar scopes to the "cab" of the tower, where the controller handles aircraft by sight and radio contact. The tower is preferred by some because of the variation in jobs performed during the day.

The air route center controller spends the work day, or night, inside a building without outside reference. The work shift is spent talking with pilots, while watching the representation of the pilot's aircraft on a radar screen. The only variation is working different sectors of airspace. Some controllers who rise to training and supervisory levels may spend time training other controllers.

The flight service controller has the greatest variety of activity. He or she assists pilots in preflight briefings, talks with pilots over the radio and telephone, assists in emergencies, helps lost pilots find a safe airport, and generally acts as a public relations person for safer flight. The controller in all of the facilities must be quite adept at operating a computer terminal.

SALARY

The ATC specialist will earn a salary that is second only to the captain with a major airline. Upon completion of the schooling at the ATC Academy, the controller will normally begin work at a government service salary schedule level of GS-7. This figure is currently $20,195 per year. As the controller progresses toward the full performance level (FPL), salary increases will come about every six months. Within five years, and upon reaching the FPL, the controller should be at a base salary of somewhere between $50,000 and $60,000. The rate of pay for the controller in the enroute center is higher than in the FSS and the tower. The tower option is divided into five levels based upon the amount of activity at the tower. Level five affords the highest pay rate. Level five towers are those found at airports like Atlanta, Chicago, Los

Angeles, and Dallas-Fort Worth. The controller receives *premium pay* (additional pay) for shift work, weekends, and holidays, which will substantially increase earnings.

EMPLOYMENT OUTLOOK

In 1981, President Ronald Reagan fired 11,000 air traffic controllers who had gone on strike in violation of federal law, which prohibits such work stoppages. Since that time, the need for ATC personnel has been tremendous. The system is recovering, but it has taken several years to do so. The FAA is still seeking several hundred people each year to train as controllers. Impending retirement of senior controllers, and the need to replace those who take medical retirement, will continue to make ATC an excellent choice for those who have the aptitude and psychological substance to qualify.

THE BOTTOM LINE

ATC affords an excellent opportunity for a satisfying career with superb financial reward. It takes a particular kind of person to pass the rigorous screening and training required. However, you are assured of a special place in life if you qualify. A person must not have reached the 31st birthday in order to be considered for the tower and enroute center positions. The FSS controller may be older. Rapid increases in base salary occur with additional training and proficiency. A person can hardly be closer to aviation than by being an air traffic controller.

FAA Operations and Maintenance Inspection

There are several positions within the FAA that are associated with performing inspections. The requirements and the duties are quite varied, yet fall into basically four major categories:

1. Operations inspectors: pilots who perform duties primarily associated with evaluating other pilots.
2. Maintenance inspectors: perform inspections of technicians and facilities where maintenance is performed.
3. Avionics inspectors: evaluate avionics technicians and their workplaces.
4. Manufacturing inspectors: work with the companies that develop and build airline and general aviation aircraft.

Operations inspectors. These FAA employees operate in two spheres of activity. One group works with air carrier operations and the other group within the general aviation system.

The air carrier inspector has responsibility for scheduled air carriers, supplemental carriers, air travel clubs, and commercial operators that fly aircraft weighing over 12,500 pounds. The general aviation inspector has responsibility for examining pilots and flight instructors and evaluating pilot training schools. Both types of inspectors investigate accidents. Both must be highly qualified pilots.

Maintenance inspectors. The duties of these inspectors involve evaluating maintenance technicians, repair facilities, maintenance programs of training schools, and maintenance programs of either general aviation operators or air carrier operators. These inspectors are normally separated in the same manner as the operations inspectors, working either with air carriers or with general aviation operators.

Avionics inspectors. These inspectors evaluate avionics technicians and repair facilities, inspect aircraft for compliance with regulations, and investigate and report on accidents, incidents, and violations. They specialize in either general aviation or air carrier-type operations. The inspectors must have three years of avionics supervisory experience on the type of aircraft to be inspected.

Manufacturing inspectors. These inspectors have the responsibility of administering and enforcing safety regulations and standards for the production of aircraft. The FAA inspector is included by the manufacturer early in the plans for new aircraft and continues to monitor the development throughout the manufacturing and testing of the airplane, until the airplane receives FAA certification. This is a costly process for the manufacturer and one in which it is important that the FAA be involved from the beginning.

This inspector must have a background in quality control methods and in the manufacturing of aircraft, engines, or components. The inspector must be able to evaluate whether the aircraft meets design specifications and airworthiness standards before a certificate may be authorized. He or she may also be involved in approving modified, import, military surplus, and home-built aircraft.

The inspectors in all of the aforementioned categories may work out of district FAA offices or manufacturing inspection district offices. Some may work in Oklahoma City at the National Field Office of Aviation Standards. There are approximately 90 flight standards district offices and some 40 manufacturing inspection district offices throughout the United States.

The inspector's knowledge and experience are the foundation upon which our system of air safety regulation depends. Inspectors will continue to receive recurrent training throughout their career.

•

SALARY

FAA inspectors are normally hired at a GS level between 9 and 11, although some, because of extensive experience and certification, may be hired as high as a GS-15. GS-9 is presently $24,705. GS-11 is $29,891. There are 10 steps within the government service pay scale for each GS level. A GS-11 could earn

$38,855 at step 10. The current maximum basic pay under the government pay scale is $78,200. Additional pay is given for shift work, holidays, and weekends.

EMPLOYMENT OUTLOOK

Congress has recently authorized the hiring of 300 safety inspectors. The position of inspector is not a position that one can rely on being available with consistency. Some years are good hire years, others are not. Since inspectors normally come from other aviation careers into the FAA, it makes good sense to retain the aviation job you have and wait to make application for the position of inspector until the announcement of hiring occurs.

THE BOTTOM LINE

The job of an FAA safety inspector is one that is never routine. Almost every day is different from the previous day. Depending upon which category of inspector one may be, he or she is likely to visit a training school one day, conduct a line check of pilots at an air show the following day, inspect the facilities of a major carrier another day, and ride in the jump seat of a 747-400 to review the crew coordination on a subsequent day. Of course there is plenty of paperwork. One inspector indicated that a person would have about two days of paperwork for each day in the field. An inspector must be able to communicate well, both verbally and in writing.

The pay is very good. The working conditions are usually superb, except perhaps when investigating an accident. Recurrent training keeps the inspector on the cutting edge of technological change. The operations inspector, for example, may go to school several times per year to maintain currency on different aircraft, such as a corporate jet, a jet helicopter, or a turboprop twin.

Engineering and Testing

ENGINEERING AND ENGINEERING AIDES

The FAA must have the services of engineers and those who work with engineers. Almost every type of engineer is needed by the FAA, but particularly the aeronautical, electrical, electronic, mechanical, and civil engineer. The engineer works on research and development problems associated with aviation, such as aircraft noise, instrument landing systems, airport construction, and especially those elements that will enhance flight safety in the air or on the ground.

EDUCATION

The engineer will have graduated from an accredited engineering college or university. The engineer may already have gained valuable work experience prior to joining the FAA. Most engineering schools provide cooperative education opportunities for their students. This allows the engineer to gain excellent work skills while attending college.

The engineering aide and engineering technician assist the FAA engineer by drafting plans, conducting necessary tests under the guidance of the engineer, setting up laboratory equipment, and assisting in preparing technical reports. The technician is normally senior to the aide and will be hired at a higher GS pay level. The duties required of the technician normally involve more responsibility than those of the aide.

The technician and the aide may receive their formal education within a college, a technical institute, or a private proprietary school. The engineering technician may be certified by the Institute for Certification of Engineering Technicians (ICET). Graduation from a school recognized by ICET will normally assure a technician of greater acceptance within the industry.

WORKING CONDITIONS

Most work is conducted inside within a laboratory or outside supervising or observing tests on aircraft and components. Some travel is necessary in order to gather information, observe tests at other facilities, or consult with airport administrators about local problems. Engineers and their assistants may work at FAA Headquarters in Washington, D.C.; at the FAA Technical Center in Atlantic City, N.J.; at NASA sites throughout the United States; at certain military bases; or at one of the eight regional FAA offices.

SALARY

Engineers may be hired at a level as low as GS-5, which would be very unusual, and as high as GS-14, depending upon past experience and educational background. It would be common that one be hired closer to the GS-14 than the GS-5. The GS-14 in step 1 earns around $50,342 per year. This would be for a normal 40-hour week. Additional compensation is earned for unusual working conditions.

Technicians and aides may be hired at levels from GS-1 up to GS-12, with the technician being employed at the higher level. They also work a 40-hour week. Some travel may be required, but not as frequently as for the engineer. Federal jobs allow a liberal travel allowance for trips required of an employee's particular position. You may see this referred to as *per diem*.

EMPLOYMENT OUTLOOK

The FAA, like many other government and nongovernment organizations, hires engineers on a rather consistent basis. The employment of technicians and aides usually is much less consistent. You must keep in contact with the FAA district office to learn of announcements for aides and technicians. Employment with the FAA, like with many other government entities, requires considerable patience on the part of the applicant. It is not unusual for the process to take from nine months to a year—even when they want you.

Working in engineering with the FAA can be exciting and very rewarding. You are compensated well, are constantly on the frontier of change in aviation, and usually work in pleasing surroundings. If you have a particular penchant for design, modification, or innovation, this may be just the place for an interesting aviation career.

Civil Aviation Security Specialist

The person occupying this particular position is normally referred to as a federal air marshall. There are similarities between the duties of this job and those found in the FBI and the Secret Service. The marshall is normally armed, must go through an extensive phase of training in security measures, and must be in top physical conditions. Considerable travel is required. The job of the marshall is to provide air travel security for everyone who flies with the airlines.

EDUCATION

No specific educational requirement is listed for this position. However, education may be used in lieu of general experience requirements. Recent college graduates are encouraged to apply. The hiring procedure can be hastened if you have a grade point of at least 3.5 on a 4.0 system, a demanding requirement by anyone's yardstick.

General experience requirements give some insight into the type of education desired in order to develop the necessary skills. You should have experience which will assure that you can understand legal provisions, regulations, and administrative procedures and be able to apply them. You also must have the ability to analyze written and numerical data, draw conclusions, and make decisions. The ability to communicate effectively, orally and in writing, is obviously required, as it would be of nearly any position in today's workplace.

WORKING CONDITIONS

The federal air marshall travels approximately 60 percent of the time on the job. The FAA normally assigns most employees to a specific region, and about 75 percent of the travel will be to facilities within that region. The remaining 25 percent may be throughout the world as needed. The marshall can be sent to any country to which a U.S. airline travels. That includes nearly all of the world's countries.

Much of what the marshall does is considered classified information and is not available to the general public. Most of the job will be concerned with whether airports and airlines are complying with FAA regulations regarding baggage, individuals, transportation of hazardous materials, and general security measures. Additional work involves investigations of inflight incidents of hijacking, bomb threats or explosions, illegal activities, and improper conduct in or around FAA facilities.

The marshal is involved in reviewing a great amount of paperwork that is required to comply with federal aviation regulations. The marshall also travels aboard designated flights to review the security measures involved and spends a considerable amount of time in trying to "crack" the security involved in boarding a plane without proper clearance. The marshall may also try to pass through airport security while carrying a weapon, such as a gun or an illegal knife, to test the effectivness of the security system. This is probably some of the more fun activity of the marshall, although not something to be taken lightly.

Training of the federal air marshall is also part of the working conditions, because much time is spent in training. The marshall undergoes a basic training program of 11 weeks in Arizona. This is followed by four two-week training sessions at the FAA Academy in Oklahoma City. Three hours of physical training are required each week throughout the marshall's career.

The marshall must also engage in weapons firing each month and will go back to Arizona every six months for a recurrent one-week training program. You can see that this is a most demanding job. The marshall also submits to random drug testing on a frquent basis. The marshall must take a complete physical examination each year, similar in nature to the Class II Airman's Medical Certificate. If over 40 years of age, the marshall will undergo an annual electrocardiogram (EKG) to determine heart condition.

SALARY

Specialized experience of the applicant will determine the entering salary. One year of such experience allows the federal air marshall to enter at the GS-7 grade, two years at the GS-9, and three years at the GS-11 or GS-12 level. The job announcement outlines the various experiences that qualify as specialized experience. Experience as a compliance inspector, investigator, analyst, planner, auditor, or investigative journalist may qualify. Experience in legal work or specific knowledge of the laws and regulations in assessing compliance are areas that are considered important.

The new federal air marshall is normally brought into the security division as a GS-7, at a salary of roughly $20,195. You may expect to rise to $24,705 after one year, $29,891 after two years, and—beginning the fourth year,—reach the journeyman level of around $35,825 per year. Salary differs with overtime, supplements for being away from home, other government service credits, and a host of other situations which affect rates of pay.

EMPLOYMENT OUTLOOK

The FAA has established a federal register for marshalls in much the same manner as for other FAA positions. Announcements may be obtained from the Office of Personnel Management or from local offices of the FAA. A competitive examination is required of those who are not college graduates with a 3.5 grade point average or who have not graduated in the top 10 percent of their college class. Position on the register is determined by your test score and whether you have a veteran's preference (10 points are added to the score of the qualifying veteran). The number of marshalls hired will vary each year. A region of the FAA may hire as many as 30 new marshalls in a given year, while other regions may hire none.

THE BOTTOM LINE

The Federal Air Marshall's job is one of great importance to the nation. More than 450 million people fly within the United States each year. The marshall protects these people from external threat by assuring that airports and airlines engage in an active security program of compliance with federal regulations. The present job outlook is good. The pay is satisfactory the first few years and becomes quite good from about year four on. The job involves travel and is quite exciting for a person who likes to travel.

However, the job announcement is quite clear that the marshall, especially when in the field, may be subject to high risk of personal injury, either in self-defense or in defense of others. This is not a warning to take lightly. Other field work, while perhaps not dangerous, is quite physically demanding. The amount of time spent away from home also may be disruptive to family life. But if you would like to travel extensively, would like to carry a firearm, appreciate physically demanding work, can communicate well, and enjoy interacting with others, being a marshall may be for you.

Other FAA Positions

The FAA hires numerous individuals who do not have education or experience directly related to aviation. The FAA employs physicians who study the effects of flying on the human body, who help establish standards for the three classes of FAA medical examination, and who conduct research into stress related to careers such as air traffic control.

The FAA utilizes lawyers who represent the FAA in legal matters, who help write FAA regulations, and who assist in developing agreements with foreign airlines.

The FAA also hires urban planners, airport safety specialists, economists, mathematicians, budget analysts, property and material managers, accountants, and others. Of course, a large organization must have a variety of workers such as secretaries, librarians, typists, mail clerks, computer programmers and operators, and those with an assortment of skills. Whatever your aspiration is in terms of a career, the FAA may be an excellent place for you to apply those skills you learn.

In addition to working for the federal government, one can find excellent positions with state governments and with associations at the national level. Let's look at two examples.

STATE AERONAUTICS AGENCIES

Each state has an aeronautics office, commission, agency, or some form of state regulatory unit which, among other functions, is the conduit for state funds to airports and aviation-related functions within the state. The state unit may be as small as one person or as large as several dozen employees. In addition to approving grants to airports for construction, maintenance, and runway improvement, some aeronautics offices are responsible for flying the governor, the cabinet, and other state dignitaries. Some states fund workshops for teachers, where they can learn about the benefits of aviation and pass the information on to their students. Some states offer youth camps, in cooperation with Scouts or the Civil Air Patrol, where young people can learn about aviation careers, the history of aviation, and rocketry. The young person may begin flying, gliding, or ballooning at such camps.

If the aeronautics office is one of the state's larger units, it will have several divisions. One division may consist of engineering, which helps to plan and develop airports and airport expansion. Another division may consist of professional pilots and maintenance technicians who fly and maintain a fleet of airplanes. Yet another division may consist of employees who work with air pollution and noise abatement procedures at the major carrier airports. Each office will have an administrative division, which handles the reams of paperwork associated with millions of aviation user-tax dollars that are dedicated to improving the aviation infrastructure. In most states, the office uses funds collected exclusively from taxes paid on airline tickets and aviation fuel sold. Thus, such services in no way take away from highways, schools, or the social welfare system.

Because of the unique nature of each state aeronautics office, it is not possible to describe all of the potential career opportunities available. Each state is organized in a different manner. Some aeronautics offices are autonomous. Some are under the state department of transportation. In some states, the governor and state officials are transported by the state's air national guard. You will need to check with your state to determine what career opportunities exist.

The kinds of positions for which you may prepare yourself in order to work for a state aeronautics agency are: pilot, maintenance and avionics technician, civil engineer, draftsperson, administrator, aerospace educator, environmental engineer, and accountant, to list a few.

It is alway helpful to develop good communication skills, regardless of the position you choose to hold. At some point in your career, you may speak before groups, or have to defend your operational budget or present your ideas to committees for approval. Once you feel comfortable speaking before peers, you will be much more effective in defending ideas before supervisors or the boss.

National Association of State Aviation Officials

The National Association of State Aviation Officials (NASAO) is the organization which represents and lobbies for the various state aeronautics offices. Several professional positions exist in NASAO, which involve research, public relations, and dealing with the U.S. Congress, with airports, and others. In recent years, NASAO has offered an internship program in the Washington, D.C. headquarters, which really is a full-time paid position for a specific period of time, usually one year. This provides an excellent opportunity for the newly graduated aviation management major.

States provide a regulatory function for aviation organizations that operate only within the state. The FAA obviously regulates aviation within the United States. NASAO assists in preventing conflicting legislation between state and federal agencies, as well as promoting uniformity among the laws and regulations of the various states.

As you seek a career in aerospace, look at state and federal organizations and governments. They offer outstanding opportunities for learning, for a career of service, and for a stimulating way of life.

CHAPTER 7

AEROSPACE MANUFACTURING

The aerospace manufacturing industry in the United States consists of approximately 80 major firms. These companies are engaged in designing, developing, manufacturing, and selling airframes, engines, avionics, and components. All of these items are necessary to fly and maintain the hundreds of different aerospace vehicles used around the world.

One of the major contributions of the aerospace industry is that it provides a favorable balance of payments between the United States and other countries—that is, we sell more aerospace products to other counties than we import. The only other U.S. industry to enjoy such a favorable balance is agriculture. Aerospace sales amounted to nearly $130 billion in 1988 and are projected to rise to $180 billion to 1992. The United States buys more than 60 percent of the goods produced by U.S. aerospace manufacturers each year.

Since the manufacturing area is so broad and requires such a diversity of talent and skill, it is impossible to list all of the positions available. Thus, this chapter will be concerned more with describing the major divisions of the industry, where the production facilities are located, some specific jobs for which you may apply, and what the outlook for the industry is into the 1990s.

MANUFACTURING OF MAJOR-CARRIER AIRCRAFT

The Big Three

The three major-carrier aircraft manufacturers in the United States for years were—in order—Boeing, McDonnell Douglas, and Lockheed. Lockheed has virtually stopped producing commercial air carriers and is concentrating on military aircraft and spacecraft. Not only was Lockheed replaced worldwide by Airbus Industries from Europe, but McDonnell Douglas also has slipped behind Airbus, now ranking third after Boeing and Airbus. Thus, the Big Three in the United States have become the Big Two for purposes of producing large civilian airliners.

BOEING

The Boeing Aircraft Company has dominated the market for large airliners for several years. In 1988, Boeing controlled 58 percent of the market in aircraft orders and 62 percent in dollar value. The worldwide aircraft market through the year 2005 is projected to be worth over $500 billion. Nearly $100 billion worth of aircraft are already on order. The average annual delivery for the next several years is projected at a value of $30 billion. While Boeing will not manufacture all of these, it will have a significant share.

Boeing's main plants are located in Auburn, Everett, and Seattle, Washington. It also has facilities in Portland, Oregon. The mainstays of Boeing's production will continue to be the 737, 747, 757, and 767. These are medium-to-long-range aircraft, the kind of planes that carry up to several hundred passengers and may fly overseas. Boeing has production facilities in many locations throughout the United States and in some foreign countries. However, if you want to work on the major airframes, you'll have to go to Washington.

It is ironic that Boeing considered leaving the commercial aircraft market in the 1960s because of poor sales. The final aircraft design it planned to introduce was the B-727. This plane soon became the world's most popular airliner, with sales nearing 2,000 units. The 727 pulled Boeing out of deep debt and assured the company of a place in history. The B-737 has already exceeded the number of 727's produced. Due to the tremendous increase in overseas travel, and because of the great distances involved, the B-747 has finally come into its own. Pacific nations like Japan, Korea, Singapore, and Thailand are buying dozens of the free world's largest airliner.

MCDONNELL DOUGLAS

McDonnell Douglas has been successful with the short-route model DC-9, owned and flown by almost every airline in the world. It was designed for approximately 100 passengers and for routes that were in the vicinity of two hours or less. It became particularly popular with the "hub-and-spoke" concept immediately following deregulation of the airlines, although it also had been in great use prior to that time. The hub-and-spoke concept involves an airline basing the majority of its fleet in one location, with most planes flying into, out of, or through this "hub" airport. On a map, these routes appear as "spokes" radiating from the hub. Some major carriers have several hubs. Among the more well-known hubs are those for United Airlines in Chicago, American in Dallas, and Delta in Atlanta.

The DC-9 has gone through several modifications. The current Super-80 is basically a design change of the older DC-9 and enjoys great popularity. It is quiet, fast, climbs well, and is flown with a two-person crew. Salt Lake City, Utah, has become a major subassembly location for the MD-80. The newer MD-90 currently is offered in one model, but it is anticipated that a shorter and longer version may be offered by 1991.

McDonnell Douglas is headquartered in St. Louis, Missouri. Somewhat like Boeing, it has plants in various locations. The new MD-11 is produced in Long Beach, California, and may become one of the major sellers in the long-range market. It is smaller than the 747, but it carries about 323 passengers, plus freight, on long overseas legs or coast-to-coast. The MD-11 is the replacement for the popular DC-10. Douglas has had some major setbacks in development and production in recent years.

The company has a mix of about half-and-half between military and civilian products. So long as the economy is positive and aircraft sales are brisk, McDonnell Douglas should do fine. The company's aircraft are sold out through 1995. Many businesses of all kinds would be enviable of that position.

LOCKHEED

Lockheed, headquartered in Burbank, California, is an old name in large airliner production. Lockheed has chosen to put aside that heritage in favor of concentrating on major military aircraft and spacecraft. The last commercial success of Lockheed was the L-1011 Tristar, a medium-to-long-range airplane that carried between 250 and 400 passengers. The L-1011 has been known as "the pilot's airplane." Airline pilots love this aircraft, primarily for its handling ability. Lockheed has modified one of its successful military transport airplanes, the C-130, into a short-field passenger airplane. The civilian version will be sold primarily to Third World countries because of its ability to land on short runways in lesser-developed areas. The C-130 has been built in a cargo version for some time. It is a turboprop, four-engine plane. Lockheed's military aircraft will be discussed further in a later section of this chapter.

GENERAL AVIATION MANUFACTURING

Twelve years ago the general aviation (GA) industry was building and selling over 17,000 units per year. The absolute bottom dropped out beginning in 1979, and even more dramatically in 1982. By 1986, fewer than 1,500 units per year were being produced by U.S. firms. Interestingly, the total dollar value dropped by only 50 percent, while production declined by over 90 percent, because the majority of remaining production was for the more expensive airplanes. Around 33 percent of the U.S. production in GA is exported to other countries each year.

Airplanes during the 1980s were also increasing in price by quantum leaps, due in large part to product liability costs associated with the American tendency to take the manufacturer to court every time one of its planes had an accident. What is ironic is that while people became more inclined to file lawsuits, the GA industry was at the same time experiencing a decrease of 50 percent in accidents. Fatal accidents also dropped by nearly 50 percent. Corporate aviation accident rates are the lowest in general aviation and closely rival airline rates.

The Big Five

The major U.S. GA manufacturers are Cessna, Learjet, Beech, Gulfstream, and Piper. There are other manufacturers, of course, but their production does not compare to the top five.

Building aircraft is a labor-intensive industry. It requires great skill learned over years of apprenticeship and practice. Overall, the industry was devastated by the drop in production during the 1980s. Cessna alone went from more than 20,000 workers to fewer than 5,000. That is a tremendous loss of great knowledge and skill.

CESSNA

Cessna has become the leading producer of executive jets in the world. The Cessna Citation, now into its fifth model, is popular because of price, ease of operation, and its ability to get into smaller airports. It is a good "step-up" aircraft from the twin turboprop. Many Citation owners cooperate each year by flying Special Olympics participants to their national meet. It is quite a sight to view over a hundred Citations arriving at one airport.

LEARJET

The Learjet Corporation has the second most popular turbojet in operation today. Several Lear models are produced, competing for the low-end market as well as the high-medium market. Lear was the first corporate jet manufactured for the corporate market. William Lear, who conceived the Learjet, also invented the car stereo and several other major items. The company has headquarters in Wichita, Kansas.

BEECH

Beech Aircraft Corporation has been the leading producer of turboprop executive aircraft for years. The company purchased the patents for the Mitsubishi Diamond, a turbojet aircraft, and now produces the Beechjet, along with the various King Air turboprop models.

GULFSTREAM

Gulfstream builds airplanes for the top-of-the-line market. The Gulfstream IV is the most expensive corporate jet built. It competes with the Falcon from France and the Challenger from Canada. Depending upon the interior, either of these aircraft can range from $16 million to over $24 million apiece. Gulfstream's "green" aircraft (without interior and paint) still remains the most expensive basic airplane. Some of the major airline-type manufacturers make an occasional airliner for personal or corporate use. These would be more expensive, however. They are rare and are not consistently produced. Gulfstream is located in Savannah, Georgia.

The Sabreliner Corporation of Chesterfield, Missouri, also makes a corporate jet. However, its main source of sales has been the military.

PIPER

All of the major manufacturers dropped training aircraft from their inventory for a period of time. They tended to concentrate on large twins and turboprops or pure jet executive models. Piper, under the recent ownership of Stuart Millar, has once again added a trainer to its line. It is called the Cadet and is selling at fantastic rates. Piper also began a limited production of its famous J-3 Cub, which at one point in history was the world's leading training aircraft. Piper is headquartered in Vero Beach, Florida, having moved from its former location in Lock Haven, Pennsylvania.

EMPLOYMENT WITH MANUFACTURERS OF U.S. AIRCRAFT

We have been discussing primarily the development and building of the major-carrier airplane and the top manufacturers of corporate and training aircraft. By doing so, we risk leaving out some other important firms that have been developing excellent airplanes for decades. However, the production of such airplanes is somewhat like the automobile production of Ferrari or Lamborghini: very few are built each year. Our interest is to provide information which will give you the best opportunity for employment, and that is normally with the larger companies that hire the most people.

Education

Aircraft manufacturers seek the most highly qualified and educated person they can attract, just as in all other areas of aerospace. Everyone likes to hire experienced and skilled craftworkers. However, companies are realistic and understand that their needs are often greater than the supply of such workers. A high school diploma normally is required, unless you have a skill or trade that is of particular value to the manufacturer. College or technical school training is recommended.

Manufacturers hire a great number of professionals each year. Aeronautical and industrial engineers, computer specialists, supervisory personnel, aircraft safety specialists, and numerous other workers in various job categories make up some of the hiring needs. Administrative positions—usually requiring a college degree—have such titles as contracts administrator, materials manager, compliance director, and production manager.

Certification

We have said previously that the aerospace industry is one of the most regulated industries in existence. Since the Federal Aviation Administration (FAA) has the certification responsibility for all U.S.-manufactured aircraft, it stands to reason that manufacturers like to hire workers who are also FAA-certified. In fact, aircraft manufacturers compete with the FAA, the airlines, and general aviation for certified maintenance and avionics technicians. The aircraft industry has considerable need for people trained or experienced in metal work. The person who can form, weld, size, or inspect metal forming can expect a welcome reception by the aircraft industry.

Composite materials are becoming popular in constructing airplanes of all types. Many of the major-carrier aircraft have some composite surfaces. Some general aviation aircraft are built exclusively from composite materials, although these tend to be found more in the home-built category. Preparing yourself to work with composite materials may assure you a place in this industry.

Working Conditions

Manufacturing of almost any description can be quite demanding, both physically and psychologically. Employees often work near large machines, loud riveting guns, and cranes that may be constantly moving large items overhead. Hugh assembly plants may not have ideal climatic conditions, being either too hot or too cold for comfort. Many of the plants hire thousands of workers and operate several shifts. This may mean walking a great distance from a parking place into the plant, working a night shift, and interacting with all kinds of people. Strikes are not uncommon in unionized plants, causing workers to lose several weeks of pay when contract negotiations are terminated. Within some plants, the work ethic seems of little importance, as some workers do not do their share of the work. There even have been reports of workers who were required to falsify information related to work on government contracts.

You can perceive these conditions as negative and find the manufacturing workplace a hostile environment in which to earn a living. On the other hand, you might find a challenge in such circumstances and could enjoy bringing creativity and innovation to the job site. There are many positive aspects to working in the manufacturing industry. The pay is usually good, the benefits superb, and the opportunity for continued employment fair. There have been large employment swings in this industry, depending upon the national economy, the defense buildup, and the extent to which new technology has been accepted by the potential purchaser. However, if you are skilled in a particularly needed area, long term layoffs will not likely affect you.

Salary

Rates of pay will vary depending upon whether one is skilled, certified, or experienced as well as whether one is *salaried* or *classified,* salaried being those in administration and classified usually being those who are blue-collar or hourly workers. Additional factors affecting pay will be the economic condition of the company, the geographical region of the nation in which the company is located, and, to some degree, whether the company is unionized. There are nonunion companies in which pay and benefits exceed those of unionized plants, but this is still somewhat rare.

Some examples of current pay rates for a large aircraft manufacturer in the Southeast will give you an idea of how the industry compensates its employees. Table 7.1 represents beginning hourly rates for each classification. Pay increases are given every six months. At the end of three years, the utility person will be earning $14.25 per hour. If the utility person is attending school or learning a trade, it is possible that he or she could change classification, and move to a different labor grade.

Table 7.1

Rates of Pay for Company X Southeast United States

Job Classification	Beginning Hourly Rate
Utility person	$8.60
Metal sizing	8.87
Shop dispatcher	8.92
Form operator	9.04
Inspector	9.23
Electrician	9.70

Professional employees normally are on a fixed salary, which may change, depending upon how the supervisor rates the employee or perhaps what kind of profit margin the company had the previous year. Beginning salaries for professional employees can vary by several thousand dollars per year. A college graduate may begin as a contracts administrator for around $18,000 per year with one company. Another company across town may employ a graduate with a degree in technology as a space packaging engineer for $31,000. Companies associated with military and space manufacturing will call almost everyone an engineer, whether or not they actually have an engineering degree. It looks better on paper. The technologist may be performing the duties formerly accomplished by an engineer. There is a tendency for companies to hire engineers for positions that do not require an engineer. Some forward-looking companies are realizing that college graduates with technology degrees often can perform tasks once thought to be the province of engineers only. The technology graduate will likely be more satisfied than an engineer, who may feel underemployed while performing routine tasks.

The college graduate who is qualified to work for an aircraft manufacturer will likely have a starting salary in the low to mid-twenties. The engineer will probably begin in the high-twenties to low-thirties. Experienced workers may command as much as a one-third increase when changing companies. There is a tendency within this industry to "raid" other companies for certain skill levels or administrative expertise.

Employment Outlook

Nearly everyone is happy that most of the world's major military powers are at peace and are scaling back on defense spending. However, this state of affairs is expected to impact manufacturing companies that depend heavily on military contracts. Experts in the field tend to believe that civil aircraft manufacturing and an anticipated escalation of the space program will offset such military cutbacks for the industry as a whole. Some impact will be felt by those working within the defense industry. This is, however, an industry that will be around throughout our lifetime. Perhaps as you decide upon a career, you should give thought to developing skills and expertise which are usable within the broad manufacturing field.

The Bottom Line

The manufacturing industry is a gigantic industry. It generates billions of dollars, employs hundreds of thousands of people, and is responsible for helping the nation maintain somewhat of a balance of trade with other nations. The industry employs workers to provide all types of skills, trades, expertise, and professional services. There are both positive and negative sides to working within the industry. On the one hand, the pay can be good. You may choose to live in a variety of states and still work in this industry. The work itself can be exciting and challenging. On the other hand, this field is subject to fluctuations in employment, due primarily to the economic health of the nation and the state of foreign affairs. Some people might find the workplace uncomfortable and the work itself tedious. Your own feelings about the aspects of the work will determine whether it is a good field for you.

AIRCRAFT ENGINE MANUFACTURERS

Early developers of flying machines often had to build their own engines because either what they needed was not available, or general engine manufacturers did not want their name associated with those "crazy flying people." The major problem of existing engines in the early days of flight was their size and weight. The engines were massive and extremely heavy. We are fortunate that engines have progressed right along with airframes, giving us more powerful engines than normally needed to do the job. The U.S. is also a major manufacturing center for jet and reciprocating engines. Engine developers are divided by the market for which they produce, just as are the airframe manufacturers.

Air Carrier Engines

There are basically three manufacturers of engines for the major-carrier aircraft. One is General Electric (GE) of Lynn, Massachusetts. GE is supplying a large number of engines for the 747 series as well as some smaller models. The company's main competitor is Rolls-Royce of England. Pratt-Whitney of Canada also has come on strong in recent years in building large engines as well. Like several of the airframe companies, GE has plants in various locations. Some of the large buyers of major-carrier aircraft can specify which engine they prefer.

General Aviation Engines

Practically everyone is into smaller jet and reciprocating engines. In addition to the firms mentioned in the previous section, general aviation suppliers include Textron Lycoming of Williamsport, Pennsylvania; Teledyne Continental of Mobile, Alabama; and the Allison Division of General Motors. Continental and Lycoming are the principal manufacturers of piston engines for the small training aircraft.

Education and Employment Outlook

If you want to work for an engine manufacturer, you should have a good background in engine mechanics. Some of the same skills are needed as found in airframe manufacturing. One element of continued production by engine makers is that an engine usually wears out well before the airframe does. This requires either new engines or remanufactured ones. The majority of smaller engine manufacturers have been bought by larger conglomerates, which tends to give greater stability to workers. The outlook for engine manufacturing of both air carrier and general aviation engines appears quite solid.

MILITARY AND SPACE MANUFACTURING

Many of the major manufacturers of air carrier aircraft and engines also are involved in developing and building defense and space vehicles. There are several companies which concentrate almost exclusively on the latter. A few of the companies are General Dynamics, LTV Corporation, Lockheed, Rockwell, Thiokol, and TRW.

One of the problems associated with the military industrial base is that the United States has been sliding in high technology leadership for several years. At the same time, foreign countries have been increasing their abilities in military and space vehicles and weapons. Only the strong, multicompany conglomerates could continue to successfully exist. Such companies often hire—and subsequently lay off—thousands of workers at a time, depending upon government contracts. The current peace initiatives of much of the world may further depress the military side of the manufacturing industry. Space exploration, civil transport, and other innovative means of transportation may take up the slack from a military employment downturn.

Space limitations in this book do not permit us to fully explore the military and space manufacturing industry. There are many similarities between this portion of the industry and that which was described in the aircraft and engine manufacturing sections. The major difference is the user of the product. The U.S. government buys the majority of military and space components. Such products also are sold to many foreign nations with which the United States maintains good relations. The U.S. presently is cooperating with some other nations in building military products for joint use. Japan, the European Space Community, and Canada cooperate on space development. The future of space exploration may well be a collective effort.

For many portions of the military industry, a security clearance is required. This involves a thorough investigation of your past activities, associations, and loyalty to the United States. Such clearances involve the lowest level—called confidential—up to top secret, depending upon the security involved regarding the systems with which you will work. One of the most important items to remember for your future is this: If you do drugs, you will not do anything in the aerospace industry, especially in jobs involved with military production.

CHAPTER 8

MILITARY AEROSPACE

The military provides excellent career opportunities for the aviation/space enthusiast. Practically every skill needed in civilian aviation is also needed by the various branches of the military. Every branch trains pilots, controls airports, maintains planes, has some involvement in the space program of the nation, and has a part in the manufacturing process of military aircraft, missiles, spacecraft, and weapon systems.

The military not only offers aviation careers, but also is an excellent training ground for future civilian aerospace careers. Many civilians who are air traffic controllers, airline pilots, airport managers, and maintenance personnel received their training in the military. The Federal Aviation Administration (FAA) has a process whereby military experience can substitute for civilian experience in obtaining pilot and maintenance certification, depending upon the level of experience achieved.

The added advantage of aerospace training in the military is that you may remain in an active reserve unit upon separating from the military. This allows you to maintain military skills, receive pay and benefits while serving, develop your civilian career, and ultimately receive excellent retirement benefits from the military. You get the best of both worlds.

Each branch of the military substantially trains its own aerospace workers and professionals. Some people view this as unnecessary and a duplication of expense. Others suggest that each branch has a different aerospace mission, hence the need for separate training. There are several similarities among the various branches. These similarities—such as salary, benefits, and employment outlook—will be considered toward the end of this chapter.

UNITED STATES AIR FORCE

The United States Air Force, hereafter referred to as the USAF, has the largest contingent of bases dedicated to aerospace. The training consists primarily of preparation for bombing, fighter engagement, air transport, satellite deployment, air-to-air refueling, reconnaissance, and transportation of the President of the United States as well as top civilian cabinet members and members of Congress on fact-finding missions.

Education

A college degree is required to become a pilot with the USAF. The preferred degree would be in engineering. However, the USAF has accepted pilot candidates from practically every college major known. The ultimate education for a USAF career would be graduation from the USAF Academy in Colorado Springs, but only the finest candidates need apply. The academy receives about 20,000 applications yearly, for an entering class of around 1,300. In addition to high test scores, a superb high school record, and some athletic ability, the candidate must have a congressional or presidential appointment. Other routes to commissioned officer status and a pilot slot are through USAF Reserve Officers Training

Corps (ROTC), offered at numerous colleges and universities around the nation. You may also apply to attend officer candidate school in the USAF.

Female pilots in the USAF may currently fly any aircraft except combat aircraft. We may see this change in the future. The North Atlantic Treaty Organization (NATO), to which the U.S. belongs, allows female combat-aircraft qualified pilots. Several of the USAF instructors in both basic and advanced jet trainers are women. It certainly isn't that women are not capable of flying high-performance combat aircraft, it is just that present U.S. law prohibits such flying. All-female crews are approved for operating some missile silos, and all-female crews have routinely flown the large four-engine C-141 jet cargo airplane. The USAF has around 1,500 women pilots.

Positions in aerospace for commissioned officers with the USAF literally fill pages and pages. The education required for such entry will depend upon the position to which you aspire. A discussion with the local recruiter will get you started toward your USAF aerospace career.

Other aerospace jobs that do not require being a commissioned officer will require only a high school diploma. The USAF will further the training of recruits going into such positions.

Working Conditions

The USAF officer and enlisted person work throughout the world, depending upon the career specialty chosen. Even within those countries where there are no USAF bases, American military personnel are assigned to U.S. embassies.

The range of working conditions in the USAF would fill a book. You may be stationed in a missile silo in Iowa, working several hundred feet below the earth's surface, or be in the test center in Ohio perfecting the latest flight simulator. Assignment may take place with the joint military space effort at Colorado Springs or may involve advanced wind-tunnel testing in Tennessee. An operational unit in Spain or Japan may require your expertise. You may have some choice of assignment, depending upon your training and the needs of the USAF.

Actual working conditions for USAF personnel are normally pleasurable, in peacetime. Many jobs are not much different from comparable civilian jobs. Of course, the military does operate around-the-clock, 365 days a year, so you will receive some night, weekend, and holiday duty. In times of meeting deadlines, you may very well work around-the-clock. During an emergency or armed conflict, you can throw the clock out the window!

The USAF wants you to continue learning. You may attend selective technical schools, command schools, or leadership schools for upper-level enlisted persons. Certain programs will allow you to complete college as an enlisted person, after which you may qualify for officer training. Such working conditions can be quite desirable.

UNITED STATES NAVY

The United States Navy, hereafter referred to as the USN, has many of the same aerospace missions as the USAF. However, many of those missions will be conducted from aircraft carriers and submarines instead of large air bases located on land. The USN does have several land bases for flight training, for long-duration overhaul and maintenance, and for technical and command schools. The Marine Corps technically reports to the USN, and during times of armed conflict or war becomes a part of the USN. However, the marines are represented by equal command on the Joint Chiefs of Staff, who advise the President on defense matters.

Education

USN officers must be college graduates, with two exceptions. Graduates of the three-year nurse diploma program and graduates of the Naval Aviation Cadet (NAVCAD) flight program will be commissioned upon completing these programs. The NAVCAD program will accept men and women who have completed two successful years of college and will enroll them in the flight program. The successful graduate may be able to complete college through a special program designed for continuing education.

The USN has an excellent program of education, beginning with the U.S. Naval Academy located in Annapolis, Maryland. The naval academy is much like those of the air force and army. The graduate receives a bachelor's degree, frequently majoring in engineering, and may take a commission as a navy ensign or marine corps second lieutenant. Approximately 1,350 candidates are accepted yearly. The navy also provides education aboard ship in many areas of the world. Enlisted personnel normally have a high school diploma, and many have experienced some level of postsecondary schooling. The educational level of all service branches is increasing.

Working Conditions

The USN enjoys a varied existence on the water, beneath the seas, and in the air. Ships that support aircraft carriers and missile-carrying submarines can be as large as a small city. Thousands of people may serve aboard a carrier. Several hundred will carry on duties aboard a sub-tender. There are machine shops on board that allow skilled workers to manufacture almost any part needed to sustain the operations of both branches.

The USN has nearly 600 ships and almost 6,000 aircraft. The one-million-strong force includes active duty and reserve officers, enlisted personnel, and civilian employees. Working conditions vary according to the assignment. Submarine missile crews can be mainly underwater for up to 70 days at a time, longer for special research programs similar to those conducted under the ice at the north pole. Aircraft carriers can be deployed for over six months and longer in times of armed conflict. Conditions can be cramped and unpleasant aboard ship, especially for enlisted persons. The workday can be exceedingly long when a carrier is constantly deploying aircraft. The exposure to wind, sea, and sun can be uncomfortable at times. The navy requires a special kind of person, one who thrives on accomplishment, challenge, stimulation, and commitment.

UNITED STATES MARINE CORPS

As mentioned previously, the United States Marine Corps technically is part of the Department of the Navy. We will look at the marine corps briefly in order to distinguish between some of the programs, assignments, and different aircraft flown. The marine is normally stationed at bases which include both navy and marine personnel. Marines are stationed aboard ship, at U.S. embassies, and at major bases like those at Quantico, Virginia, or Parris Island, South Carolina. The marine corps has one particular motto that is rather apparent, regardless of the skill or job function. They say that the person is a marine first, then secondly a pilot or whatever specialty for which the marine is trained. You may have to grab a weapon and hit the ditch if you are needed for infantry-type duties in times of an emergency!

Education

The official marine policy is "stay in school." You must be a college graduate to be commissioned. If you are a graduate of the naval academy, you may choose either the navy or the marines. Some navy ROTC programs at selected colleges also allow you to choose the marines. A popular program for receiving a marine corps commission is the platoon leader's class (PLC). A freshman or sophomore can spend two six-week terms at the officer candidate school in Quantico. A junior attends one 10-week session. Upon graduation from college, the person then receives a commission. There are two added educational options available. You may postpone active duty if you are pursuing a law degree or if you are in an aviation pilot's option. Further information on these programs is available from recruiters.

Seniors, and those having already graduated from college, may elect to attend an officer candidate class, which affords the same opportunities as for those engaged in PLC training. Superior high school students may qualify for a navy ROTC scholarship. This will provide four years of tuition, books, fees, and $100 per month for up to 40 months. Your military training will take place during the summers, with a six-week cruise aboard ship following your freshman year, four weeks of warfare specialities training following the sophomore year, and a precommission training period between the junior and senior year.

Women may qualify for a commission in the marine corps, but there are differences in the periods of training and scholarships that are available. The female marine may not become a pilot or naval flight officer (NFO) or occupy any job that could place her in a combat situation. Most of the continuing education programs available to the navy officer or enlisted person are available to the marine.

Working Conditions

The Marine Corps has the reputation of needing "a few good men"—and women—but is equally known for having the toughest training of any of the service branches, except perhaps for advanced training as a navy seal or army ranger. The marine is the first to hit the beach during wartime. The marines are usually the ones sent in to "hot spots" like the Middle East. The training required to produce such soldiers has to be hard. Not everyone can qualify to be a marine.

The other side of the coin is the opportunity to see the world and to serve in visible places like the White House, American embassies, aboard the marine helicopters that carry the President, or aboard ship traveling to distant ports.

The marine aviator flies two types of aircraft not flown by any other U.S. service branch. Marines fly the Harrier, which is a vertical take-off fighter. It is capable of supersonic speeds but also has the ability to maneuver like a helicopter. The free world's largest helicopter is also flown by the marine pilot. So if you like unique aircraft, you may qualify to be a marine and fly such innovative machines.

UNITED STATES ARMY

The U.S. Army may have the largest fleet of aircraft of all the military branches. The total inventory of active aircraft in January 1990 for army reserve, national guard, and active army units was 8,791. Of these aircraft, 94 percent were helicopters, used primarily as troop support gun platforms and for transporting air cavalry troops to the front line. The army also has a full complement of fixed-wing airplanes, used primarily to transport senior officers and to act as fire direction control for artillery and air force fighters. These army pilots are called forward air controllers (FACs). Replacement for retiring pilots, those separating from the service, or those going to administrative jobs, requires a large number of aircraft to be set aside for training. Quite a lot of army flight training is accomplished by civilian flight instructors, leaving the army officer free to fly with line units.

Education

The army seeks to recruit high school and college graduates. Many of the officers come from college or university ROTC units. A full ROTC scholarship, given to exceptional high school graduates, can amount to $20,000 or more per year, depending upon the college or university chosen by the student. The ultimate career opportunity exists when you graduate from the U.S. Military Academy at West Point, New York. Many of the most famous American generals and military tacticians have been West Point graduates. Entrance to the academy is equally competitive as are the navy and air force academies. Congressional appointment is required but does not assure acceptance.

The army, like the navy and marine corps, has a special rank related to aviation that is somewhat in-between senior enlisted and commissioned officer status. It is called warrant officer and is something of a holdover from early flight during armed conflict, when all branches allowed enlisted pilots. The warrant officer is assigned primarily to helicopter flight. In fact, the school that provides many of the helicopter pilots also provides that when the enlisted person completes the course, he or she is designated a warrant officer. This rank commands most of the respect and military courtesy of the commissioned officer. Some warrant officers may command a unit, although it does not occur with frequency. Command normally is left to commissioned officers. Warrant officers usually are required to complete at least two years of college in order to remain on active duty. Continuing education opportunities abound at most army bases, allowing one to complete a degree or a skills program that also has applicability to the civilian market.

Working Conditions

The aerospace worker in the army may be assigned to the major overhaul facility or training command such as Fort Rucker, Alabama, or to operating units like the 101st Airborne at Fort Campbell, Kentucky. Assignment to foreign posts such as South Korea or West Germany are common. Many of those associated with army aviation will spend a considerable amount of time in the field, honing military skills and learning to remain operational in the face of adversity. As with every aviation unit, needs will exist for pilots, maintenance and avionics technicians, loadmasters, gunners, air traffic controllers, and other specialties.

The soldier has 30 days of *leave* (vacation), rather good pay and benefits, respect from civilian employers when the service period is completed, and the opportunity to see some of the world. Long hours, assignment to dangerous or unpleasant places, and the strict discipline of military service isn't for everyone. However, within the army, aviation is one branch that is particularly exciting and one that can prepare you for an aerospace position in civilian life.

UNITED STATES COAST GUARD

The United States Coast Guard, herein referred to as the USCG, is a branch of the Department of Transportation during peacetime. During war, the USCG becomes a part of the U.S. Navy. The USCG performs many of the same functions as the navy. In particular, the USCG fights drug smuggling, rescues people stranded at sea, and protects U.S. ports and ships. The USCG is actually older than the USN.

Education

The USCG accepts persons between the ages of 17 and 26. The U.S. Coast Guard Academy, like other service academies, accepts high school graduates between the ages of 17 and 22. It is located in New London, Connecticut. People who possess a bachelor's degree and are between the ages of 17 and 26 may take a 17-week officer candidate course and become a commissioned coast guard officer. Other people who are licensed merchant marines, graduates of a maritime academy, former military pilots, or lawyers may become coast guard officers through other programs. Women have the same opportunity for selection as men. They serve in all classifications except those related to combat. While the women's coast guard was a separate entity during World War II, it is fully integrated today.

Working Conditions

The USCG officer or enlisted person performs many duties similar to navy personnel. During wartime, the USCG escorts merchant ships through unfriendly waters and may patrol foreign coasts to prevent enemy shipping. During the present peacetime, the USCG is heavily involved in slowing down drug traffic into the U.S. Such work can be dangerous. The USCG also establishes regulations for building oil tankers. The USCG performs an education function for boaters, teaching them the rules of safe boating. The USCG auxiliary patrols offshore to rescue stranded boats. Much of this work is performed by volunteers who fly their own aircraft in particular patterns before sundown.

Aviation plans a major role in the USCG. Airplanes of many descriptions are involved in search and rescue, long-range patrol, and iceberg location. Everything from helicopters, which can land in the water or on land, to the mammoth, four-engine Lockheed Hercules transport plane are used by the USCG.

The coast guard can be an exciting way of life. You must be prepared to work long hours during major emergencies and during search-and-rescue operations. The working conditions can be hazardous. The pay and benefits are equal to other service branches. Educational benefits are good. Retirement benefits are equally appropriate. Opportunities are available for travel to exotic places. The combination of ships and aircraft may be what you seek.

The USCG is not a large branch, as compared to other branches of the service. There are about 37,000 active USCG personnel and an additional 23,000 reserve members. Some civilian personnel are utilized, just as with other service branches. If you have an interest in the USCG, either as a uniformed member or as a civilian worker, you should contact the recruiter near you. Replacements for retiring and departing personnel must always be found.

MILITARY SALARIES AND BENEFITS

Salaries and benefits are generally the same for all branches of the armed forces. Pay grades are periodically altered by the government. Retired members of the service receive a cost-of-living increase, which retirees of most nongovernment jobs will not receive. This alone can be of considerable importance when planning for a comfortable retirement.

Current salary levels for enlisted persons range from slightly over $8,300 per year for the new recruit to $28,044 for the top grade. Additional compensation may be allowed for separate quarters, subsistence allowance, incentive pay, special allowances, hazardous pay, and flight pay. Many of these allowances are tax-free, which can measurably add to the money you keep. Certain of these allowances are for married enlisted personnel only.

Officers receive $17,330 per year starting out as a new second lieutenant and can get up to $52,841 as a colonel with 20 years of service. Pilots receive additional incentive pay ranging from $125 per month to $650 per month, depending upon the number of years of service as an aviation officer. The amount of time spent in service—referred to as *longevity*—will make a difference in salary, in addition to the rank you hold. Officers receive many of the additional benefits given to enlisted personnel, plus a uniform allowance.

Some of the military services have a problem with retaining pilots who have met their obligation. Higher pay from the airlines draws many pilots to the civilian market. Attempts to stem this tide have taken several forms. Bonus programs of up to $12,000 per year for re-enlisting continue to be in effect. Allowing pilots to fly longer, instead of being forced into administrative positions, also seems to have been important in retaining pilots. Bills have been introduced by Congress to raise pilot salaries and require longer periods of service for those trained as pilots in the future.

Additional perks for military personnel come in the form of possibly teaching at one of the service academies, or perhaps flying or working on one of the world-famous aerial demonstration teams like the Thunderbirds or Blue Angels. The army also has the Golden Knight Parachute Team, which provides exposure similar to top entertainers in the civilian market. Many of the military bases field competitive sports teams, especially in those sports associated with the Olympics.

Travel to great places all over the world can be a part of military service. If the foreign bases allow dependents, the service will pay for household goods and automobiles to be shipped to the duty station. When quarters are not available on base, housing allowances provide for the family to live in the foreign communities. This can be a tremendous adventure for a family. Foreign dependent schools normally are available for the children of service personnel. Special educational programs often are available for the service person as well as family members. Officers are particularly encouraged to continue their education through graduate degrees.

The Bottom Line

Military service can be an excellent way to receive training for future civilian work or a wonderful place to have a career. If you enter the service at a young age, you can retire before the age of 40 and still have many productive civilian years left for another career. You can enter a reserve or national guard unit and build points toward a career. The reserve or national guard officer or enlisted person can qualify for many service schools and thereby develop the abilities to rise in rank and experience. The author knows of one person who never served active duty time, except for schools; who went through pilot school, medical officer's school, special forces, and airborne training; and who is now a one-star general! You are limited only by your own initiative and abilities. Consider the military as an excellent opportunity for advancement.

NATIONAL OCEANIC AND ATMOSPHERIC ADMINISTRATION

The National Oceanic and Atmospheric Administration (NOAA) is the smallest of the uniformed services. It is listed only because it offers some aviation flight and maintenance opportunities. The officer with NOAA goes through an officer candidate program similar to that for officers of other services. The officer candidate must hold a bachelor's degree in science or engineering and meet the physical requirements. Women are accepted for any of NOAA's officer positions, as this is not an armed service and does not involve combat. Women have been on NOAA ships since 1972, involved in both diving and flying.

The newly commissioned NOAA officer must serve a tour on ship before qualifying for training as a pilot. Most assignments are for two to three years. Diver training is somewhat more available than flight opportunities. You definitely do not want to combine diving with flying! In fact, if you become a pilot and then decide to become a diver, even for fun, maintain strict discipline about avoiding flight immediately after diving. You can end up with decompression sickness, or "the bends," and wake up with a sheet over your face!

NOAA has 23 ships at sea. They operate from Norfolk, Virginia; Seattle, Washington; and other ports around the world. Officer training takes place twice a year at Fort Eustis, Virginia. Each session lasts 15 weeks. Application may be made to NOAA, 11400 Rockville Pike, Rockville, MD 20852. Advanced graduate work is recommended and is provided for the officer wishing to pursue such study.

CHAPTER 9

NATIONAL AERONAUTICS AND SPACE ADMINISTRATION (NASA)

Aeronautics and astronautics are terms that describe careers or occupations as well as the environments of the atmosphere and space. The National Aeronautics and Space Administration (NASA) is involved in developing and testing flight vehicles that operate in both environments. NASA also is responsible for studying the benefits of aeronautical and space activities and for cooperating with other nations in space and aeronautical pursuits while still preserving the role of the United States as a leader in aeronautical and space accomplishments.

NASA was created by Congress in 1958, a year after the Soviet Union launched the world's first satellite, Sputnik, into orbit around the earth. Prior to this event, the airspace of sovereign nations was considered *inviolable*—that is, not to be trespassed upon. Sputnik violated this principle every 90 minutes as it circled the globe. Many nations around the world were outraged. The United States was particularly upset, as it had been the world's technological leader for over a century and suddenly saw its biggest enemy paving the way into space. Americans seethed with resentment and embarrassment, and resolved to catch up and surpass what the Soviets had accomplished. The American education system was seen as the means to accomplish this resolve. The U.S. simply had to educate more and better scientists, engineers, and mathematicians. Those of you who seek positions in the fields of aeronautics and astronautics are the beneficiaries of this determination, born out of Cold War hostility, yet still thriving in today's era of global cooperation led by the United States and the Soviet Union.

NASA'S OCCUPATION CLASSIFICATION SYSTEM

NASA classifies work based upon what tasks workers perform, not upon what their educational background may be. Of course, your educational background dictates to a great degree what kind of work you are capable of accomplishing.

NASA has 10 major classifications or subgroups of its aerospace technology system. The life sciences division is further divided, but we will look at only the basic 10 divisions:

1. space sciences
2. life sciences
3. fluid and flight mechanics
4. materials and structures
5. propulsion systems
6. flight systems
7. measurement and instrumentation
8. data systems
9. experimental facilities, equipment, and operations
10. administration and management

Space Sciences

This area of investigation is concerned with planetary research as well as observation of distant stars, other galaxies, extraterrestrial phenomena, and solar terrestrial research. NASA scientists are interested not only in what is happening in space, or how planets and galaxies may have been formed, but also how such knowledge may relate to improving life on earth. Many of our present orbiting satellites give data on weather, crops, infestations, forest fires, and other elements of our environment, which will assist us in using and preserving that precious environment.

Interest areas. You may enjoy a career within NASA's space sciences division if you are interested in the principles of meteorology or astronomy or in the technological application of scientific inquiry. College majors in astronomy, astrophysics, geology, geophysics, mathematics, meteorology, and physics are most closely associated with such careers. NASA sites where you are more likely to be employed in space sciences are the Ames Research Center, Goddard Space Flight Center, Marshall Space Flight Center, and the Stennis Space Center. Addresses of these facilities are listed at the end of this chapter.

Life Sciences

Investigation in the life sciences is concerned with two principal areas. The first is the study of the effects of exposing biological organisms to space. The organism may be a human, a monkey, bees, or any form of life on earth that can be a part of a mission into space. Some study is conducted on earth to simulate the space environment.

The second aspect of the life sciences involves understanding the origin of life on earth. Several programs are included in researching this aspect of evolution. The life sciences workers help design life-support systems for astronauts, explore adaptive behavior of plants and organisms, design closed ecosystems for extended space travel, develop tools for humans working in space, and deal with numerous other aspects of life and travel beyond our earth.

Interest areas. The life sciences divisions of NASA hires people with background and education in anatomy, chemistry, botany, biology, physiology, geology, and other life sciences. If your interest is in the origin of life or in extraterrestrial travel, the life sciences divisions of NASA may hold interesting work for you. Employment in life sciences will more likely occur at Ames and Johnson space centers.

Fluid and Flight Mechanics

NASA is never satisfied with state-of-the-art flight mechanics. NASA is always working on the future, whether it be in aerodynamic vehicles, rocket or jet engines, or general aviation training aircraft. Motion mechanics forms a significant part of the research conducted. Automated controls and how pilots react to certain flight displays is important to the future air traffic system. NASA applies what it learns during in-flight experiments conducted in NASA aircraft.

Interest areas. Particular areas of expertise utilized by this division include engineering physics, astronautics, mechanical engineering, physics, and other physical sciences. Mathematics is acceptable if coupled with a minor in a physical science. Employment in fluid and flight mechanics occurs at all NASA locations except Stennis and NASA Headquarters.

Materials and Structures

This division is concerned with designing spacecraft materials and forming such materials into shapes that will withstand the tremendous forces of supersonic and space flight. Operation in space presents special problems that most of us never consider. How do we lubricate a space shuttle—can we use the same grease found at the local service station? Do the temperatures of space affect the spacecraft, requiring special insulation materials? If we use very heavy and very thick metals, how do we compensate for the added weight we must thrust into space? These are only a few of the questions considered by scientists and workers in this division of NASA.

Interest areas. College graduates and others with special knowledge in ceramics, physics, metallurgy, chemistry, and various branches of engineering are important to this division of NASA. Employment with NASA in materials and structures occurs at all sites except Stennis and NASA Headquarters.

Propulsion Systems

The single item which probably limited the possibility of flight until 1903 was the lack of an engine sufficient enough in power to lift the aircraft off the ground, but also lightweight. The same limitation exists for the future of flight. The projected space plane, which would transport the commercial passenger from New York to Tokyo in less than three hours, will combine both known and presently unknown principles of propulsion. Flight to other galaxies will require propulsion systems capable of much greater speeds than we can currently produce. These are a few of the propulsion problems being considered by NASA.

Interest areas. The specialist in propulsion must know about fuel-and-air mixing; heat transfer; energy conversion devices; solar, chemical, and nuclear sources of energy; and how such systems will react to space travel. A background in chemistry, physics, engineering, astronautics, or other physical science, along with an excellent foundation in mathematics, will assist you in obtaining employment with this division of NASA. Employment in propulsion systems is found more frequently at Goddard, Johnson, Kennedy, Lewis, and Marshall centers.

Flight Systems

We immediately think of a flight system as either an airplane or a propulsion system coupled with an airfoil. This is partially true, but not comprehensive enough. A flight system may be a probe, an orbiter, a payload, a launch vehicle, or even a test facility. An operational flight system is a combination of mission, payload, vehicle, instrumentation, and experimental design. There is also a lot of "what if" deliberation surrounding the operation of a flight system.

Interest areas. People with expertise in engineering, physics, mathematics, and especially computer science are necessary to the development of flight systems for NASA. Workers involved in flight systems are employed in all NASA centers except Stennis and Headquarters.

Measurement and Instrumentation

When a mission is deployed by NASA, several hundred workers sit in front of panels of instruments, as well as computers, and monitor what is happening to the launched vehicle. The myriad of dials, flashing lights, meters, and scales give specific data to the people skilled in monitoring the instruments. Feedback is received on the propulsion systems, the spacecraft itself, the astronauts, and the environment surrounding the craft. All aspects of the launch program, mission, and recovery depend upon the specialists who monitor the instruments. These specialists also design and test new instruments under all kinds of conditions, including simulation. An example of such instrumentation is a tiny radio transmitter designed to be swallowed by an astronaut to give core temperatures during a space mission.

Interest areas. Areas of study for people seeking positions in measurement and instrumentation include electronics, physics, mechanical engineering, and computer science. Measurement and instrumentation specialists are employed in all centers except Stennis and Headquarters.

Data Systems

The ability to enter space, perform work, and return safely depends upon many specialties, not the least of which is concerned with computers. The exploration of space probably could not exist without the computer technology which grew as a result of space exploration. One depends upon the other. The supercomputers—such as the Cray series, capable of such rapid speeds that people not skilled in computers cannot even understand—advance the opportunities of space exploration. Literally dozens of specialties have grown within the computer field, in large part because of the space program's needs. The fallout to the everyday world of work is becoming so commonplace that many people not only have a computer on their desk at work, but also one at home. Some even carry a small lap-top aboard airliners.

Prior to the computer sophistication of today, the development of aeronautical vehicles often took years of trial-and-error, hugely expensive tests in wind tunnels, and the risk of lives of pilots as they flight-tested the vehicles. Today, the vehicle can be drawn, tested, modified, and the flight test simulated on the computer. This saves millions of dollars and untold amounts of time. The vehicle must still be built and flight-tested, of course, but at that point many of the questions have already been answered.

Interest areas. If you enjoy working with computers and asking "what if" questions, then you may enjoy working in data systems. A combination of computer science, mathematics, and some area of physical or biological science is recommended for entering this futuristic field. Data systems employs persons at all NASA sites except Stennis and Headquarters.

Experimental Facilities, Equipment, and Operations

Engineers and technicians must have equipment to work with and an environment within which to work. This is the task of people who work within this division of NASA. They plan, design, and construct wind tunnels, cryogenic laboratories, solar collection systems, aircraft crash test facilities, and laboratories for investigating liquids and gases used in research programs. This brief list only scratches the surface of equipment and facilities needed in today's research environment.

Interest areas. Workers in this division come from aeronautical engineering, architecture, ceramics, electronics, metallurgy, and a host of other engineering disciplines. The facilities division hires workers in all locations except Stennis and Headquarters.

Administration and Management

The last word in NASA is administration. Any organization, especially one the size of NASA, must have an extensive web of management and administrative support. NASA installations are spread worldwide. Persons of every employment description work for NASA. The efforts of hundreds of workers must come together flawlessly *during* a major mission, and countless hours of coordination and interaction must *precede* a NASA mission or major experiment. All of this comes together only with the proper management and administrative support.

Interest areas. Managers tend to rise from within an organization, although some special skills may be brought in from outside. Highly skilled workers of the nature of NASA employees usually prefer that managers also be highly skilled in one of the disciplines they will supervise. This makes the manager ''legitimate'' in the eyes of the workers.

If you wish to emerge into management, you should be prepared in one of the scientific disciplines and should add courses in the behavioral sciences. Management personnel are located at all NASA sites. Those located at NASA Headquarters are normally senior level personnel, not entry-level.

TECHNICAL SUPPORT POSITIONS

All of the aforementioned classifications of NASA careers utilize a large number of professional personnel. However, they must be supported by an extensive array of technical, clerical, and crafts personnel. Many of these positions will require only high school and some postsecondary technical education. Many community colleges, technical institutes, and private proprietary schools provide the training necessary to secure a position with NASA or with a NASA contractor.

NASA has its own apprentice program for a variety of needed skills. A good high school record and an abiding interest in the technical area are prerequisites for entry into such an apprentice program. These positions are very competitive. It will serve you well to be involved during high school in science fairs, clubs, and summer programs of a scientific nature. It will not hurt to live close to one of the major NASA sites which have apprentice programs. These sites are listed at the end of this chapter.

NASA utilizes workers in electronics, optical fabrication, machine operation, metallographics, patternmaking, and numerous other skilled trades. Some of these may be entered through the apprentice program. You must take the Civil Service Examination to qualify for the apprentice program. NASA has prepared a number of career-oriented materials to share with you, at no cost to you. Just write to one of the locations listed at the end of the chapter and request career materials. You might specify which areas interest you most.

Since NASA employs many engineers and scientists, you may obtain a feel for the type of salaries paid by reviewing Chapter 4 on engineering research and development. Technicians earn much less than those who have graduated from college, but even their salaries are normally higher than the average American worker.

Clerical workers, analysts, computer programmers, receptionists, file clerks, mail clerks, and executive secretaries are all needed by NASA and NASA contractors. Whatever your line of interest or skill, there may be a position for you in the nation's space program.

NASA ASTRONAUT SELECTION AND TRAINING

Most of you reading this book will not remember a time when there were no astronauts. For the author and many of his contemporaries, flying into space once was a thing only for comic book characters, the Saturday serial at the local theater, and science-fiction nerds in the chemistry club. How far we have come!

Today, NASA routinely recruits pilots and mission specialists who wend their way into space at speeds in excess of 20,000 miles per hour. It does take a special breed of person to do this. It also takes special skills and knowledge, which can be learned in school. Do you have what it takes to make it into space?

Astronaut Selection

The first American astronauts were selected in 1959. There were seven of them. Of the ones who have survived, one became a retired navy admiral, one a senator, and one a retired major-airline president. All have become major speakers at conventions and group meetings.

Three years after the first selection process, the selection of Gemini and Apollo astronaut trainees began. Six of the original seven had flown in the Mercury project. The second group followed much the same career path to becoming astronauts as the original group. They were highly skilled in flying high-performance jet aircraft. They graduated from college with an engineering degree and were in excellent physical condition. The maximum age had been decreased from 40 to 35 and the maximum height limit increased from 5 feet 11 inches to 6 feet.

The third selection took place in 1963 and began changes that are still in place today. NASA was seeking outstanding academic qualifications. The 400 applicants had a doctorate or equivalent experience in the natural sciences, medicine, or engineering. Similar selection processes have taken place on an announced basis since this time.

Astronauts are selected from two groups today. There are pilot candidates and mission specialist candidates. The pilot candidate must have a bachelor's degree in engineering, biological or physical science, or mathematics. He or she must have at least 1,000 hours of pilot-in-command flight time in high-performance jets. Flight-test experience is highly desirable. The pilot candidate must pass NASA's rigorous Class I physical. More specific information is available directly from NASA.

The mission specialist must have a bachelor's degree in the same areas as specified for the pilot. The candidate must have three years of related experience in the field. A graduate degree is preferred and may substitute for some experience. The candidate must pass a NASA Class II physical.

Astronaut Training

The astronaut candidate remains a candidate for only a year. During that time, the astronaut candidate is evaluated on the ability to perform under zero-gravity conditions. This is accomplished while suited in a bulky space suit within the neutral buoyancy tank. The candidate also is evaluated in the laboratory and with fellow candidates. Teamwork is a must in space. Everyone's life is dependent upon every member of the team.

If the candidate survives the year of evaluation, he or she then is elevated to astronaut status. This is when the training really begins. Pilot astronauts will continue to fly aircraft that simulate characteristics of the space shuttle. They also will fly many hours of missions in the shuttle simulator, honing skills of docking, maneuvering, and reacting to simulated emergencies. The mission specialist will continue to study in the primary discipline, design space laboratory experiments, interact with contractors on payloads, attend engineering conferences, and advise other astronauts of what is taking place within their areas of responsibility. All astronauts must maintain top physical condition.

Astronauts are assigned to specific flights by means known only to NASA. Some astronauts may wait years to be assigned to a mission. Others may fly fairly soon after selection. Payloads are assigned to specific missions in relationship to what is to be accomplished. Mission specialist astronauts will conduct experiments related to their discipline, in so far as the experiment can be programmed for their flight. Astronauts depend upon payload integration engineers to train them to conduct payload experiments. These engineers work for NASA contractors and may actually be engineers or may be aerospace technology graduates who simply receive the title of engineer from their employer. They are an important link between the contractor and NASA.

As the assigned mission nears blastoff, the intensity of training picks up. More flying, more simulation, direct work with mission control, and numerous simulations of the full mission will take place in final preparation for the flight. After the mission, the astronauts take part in a debriefing that lasts a few hours or a few days. This may be followed by a few days of vacation, then back to training for the next mission. If you qualify, you may be able to shoot for the stars.

MAJOR NASA LOCATIONS IN THE UNITED STATES

NASA Headquarters
400 Maryland Avenue SW
Washington, DC 20546

Ames Research Center
NASA
Moffett Field, CA 94035

George C. Marshall Space Flight Center
NASA
Marshall Space Flight Center, AL 35812

Goddard Space Flight Center/Wallops
NASA
Greenbelt, MD 20771

John F. Kennedy Space Center
NASA
Kennedy Space Center, FL 32899

Johnson Space Center
NASA
Houston, TX 77058

Langley Research Center
NASA
Hampton, VA 23665

Lewis Research Center
NASA
21000 Brookpark Road
Cleveland, OH 44133

Stennis Space Center
NASA
SSC Station, MS 39529

CHAPTER 10

COLLEGIATE AVIATION PROGRAMS

You have learned that the education and technical knowledge necessary for a successful career in aerospace are available from a variety of sources. Colleges and universities represent only one type of education available. However, as aerospace becomes more technologically complex, there will be an even greater movement for colleges to solve problems and to prepare the subsequent generations for aerospace careers.

Engineers and people who work in astronautics, space sciences, astrophysics, and a variety of other physical sciences and mathematics are already prepared at the college level, many at the graduate levels. Major-carrier airlines are almost exclusively hiring pilots who are college graduates. Will the national and regional airlines follow suit? The Federal Aviation Administration (FAA) is considering a much greater utilization of colleges for preparing air traffic controllers, maintenance inspectors, and electronics technicians. If the movement is in the direction of more education, shouldn't you consider pursuing all the education of which you are capable?

STRUCTURE OF COLLEGIATE AVIATION

Over 500 colleges and universities in every state, as well as Puerto Rico and the District of Columbia, feature more than 1,000 aviation-related offerings. Programs range from noncredit courses of study and certificate programs to associate degree through doctorate levels. The full range of careers in aerospace are available in some form in the nation's colleges and universities.

The latest figures on aerospace programs, supplied by Educational Resources, Inc., indicate that there are 69 doctorate programs, 22 programs at the master's level, 287 at the bachelor's degree level, and 442 associate degree programs in our nation's colleges. The greatest number of graduate-level programs exist in two areas: aerospace engineering and astro/space physics. Table 10.1 summarizes the top five undergraduate degree areas.

Table 10.1
Collegiate Aviation Degree Programs

Program	Bachelor (No.)	Associate (No.)
Professional pilot	51	92
Management	62	78
Technology	24	102
Maintenance	22	95
Engineering	34	12

Academic Resources, Inc.

FAA AIRWAY SCIENCE PROGRAM

The FAA has sponsored a collegiate aviation program, called airway science, since 1981. It was designed through cooperation with the University Aviation Association. The program was developed to meet the long-term needs of the FAA and the aerospace industry at large. It is offered for managers who have requisite expertise within an aerospace field, but who also have the skills necessary to function in today's computer-based environment. Also of top priority was the need to develop future managers with interpersonal skills that were previously missing in many technically competent persons who had risen to management levels.

Participation in the program requires the university to submit a curriculum plan to the FAA for approval. The FAA recognizes only five options: electronics, aviation management, professional pilot, computer science, and aircraft maintenance management. Being one of the approved institutions makes the college eligible for grants from the FAA. Some grants are competitive. Some are directed to specific institutions. Nearly $40 million has been distributed to colleges since the program's inception. The FAA and the aerospace industry at large are recognizing that graduates from such approved programs are normally quality graduates who have had specific exposure desired by employers. Community college and technical institutes may articulate with a four-year college, but may not be approved individually. Very few of the 38 approved institutions enjoy approval of all five options. As of this writing, there are only six colleges so approved.

INTERNSHIP AND COOPERATIVE EDUCATION

A host of colleges and universities are involved with the aerospace industry in providing both work experience for students and excellent workers for the industry. Aerospace has been involved in the engineering fields for decades. Only recently has it been the practice for other areas of aerospace work to have more than token representation. The FAA currently provides cooperative education (co-op) experiences for air traffic controllers, administrative assistants, and operations personnel.

Other elements of the aerospace industry provide opportunities for flight dispatchers, ground service personnel, customer service agents, airport management interns, line service workers, flight instructors, simulator instructors, and other types of related employment.

Feedback from the aerospace industry to institutions that prepare students for an aerospace career tend to mention two items of major concern. Industry prefers workers with experience and those who can communicate well, both verbally and in written form. This information gives you the opportunity to make a decision about getting involved in an internship or co-op program before entering college. If you do, you'll have a jump on those who do not plan ahead. Where communication is concerned, you need those skills regardless of what you choose to do.

AEROSPACE PROBLEMS TO BE SOLVED

Aerospace is beset with major problems that must be solved if it is to continue its meteoric rise. An enterprising person who can come up with practical solutions will have a great place within the industry. Some of the problems are:

- international access to airports
- additional airports that will handle the future hypersonic airplane and jumbo jet
- more innovative instrument landing systems
- more efficient helicopters
- more heliports
- support for training and educating critical personnel such as pilots and maintenance technicians
- utilization of common training for military pilots and mechanics
- greater environmental safeguards near airports
- appropriate spending of aviation user fees
- government incentives for aviation entrepreneurs

- inducements for students to go into both engineering and the sciences

The list could go on and on, so get involved and help solve these and other problems.

SUMMARY COMMENTS ON AEROSPACE CAREERS

Aerospace is an exciting field. It is among the most innovative of careers. It is on the frontier of new knowledge and research. Salaries paid to workers are above the U.S. average for all career fields. The individual earning potential is among the greatest there is, when working for someone else. The majority of work is accomplished in pleasant surroundings. Benefits of working in the industry go far beyond salaries.

Workers with all kinds of talent, skills, training, and education help aerospace to be among the top U.S. industries. Quantum leaps in technology have occurred through the interaction of such workers. Greater things will come during your future work years than we might even imagine possible. However, they will not occur without effort, dedication, education and training, and a commitment to be the very best you can be.

In this author's opinion, we must reestablish the work ethic that made this nation great. A full day's work for a day's pay is required. Individual study beyond that required by teachers and schools or employers is essential. Honesty and integrity in dealing with the employer, and the employer with the contractor, is mandated. The courts, the regulators, and those who make our laws all must recommit to providing a place for the entrepreneur to thrive and to make a profit. We cannot "leave it to the other guy" to accomplish these necessary changes. It is up to each of us to get involved, to learn, to strive, and to innovate. What will you do today that will help tomorrow be better? We are not on this earth engaging in a trial run or dress rehearsal. This is our life, and we must live it to the fullest.

Admiral Don Engen, past administrator of the Federal Aviation Administration, once said, "Some people see a difficulty in every opportunity, while others see an opportunity in every difficulty." Which will it be for you?

MAJOR AIRLINE CORPORATE ADDRESSES

America West Airlines, Inc.
222 South Mill Avenue
Tempe, AZ 85281

American Airlines, Inc.
MD 908, Box 619617
DFW Airport, TX 75261

Continental Airlines Corporation
Box 4697
Houston, TX 77210

Delta Air Lines, Inc.
Box 20530
Atlanta, GA 30320

Eastern Airlines, Inc.
Miami International Airport
Miami, FL 33148

Federal Express Corporation
Box 727
Memphis, TN 38194

Northwest Airlines
Minneapolis/St. Paul Airport
St. Paul, MN 55111

Pan American World Airways, Inc.
JFK International Airport
Building 208
Jamaica, NY 11430

Southwest Airlines Company
Box 37611
Dallas, TX 75235

Trans World Airlines, Inc.
1307 Baltimore
Kansas City, MO 64105

United Airlines, Inc.
Box 66100
Chicago, IL 60666

U.S. AIR, Inc.
Washington National Airport
Washington, DC 20001

SELECTED BIBLIOGRAPHY

Bacon, Harold R., Michael D. Schrier, Patricia F. McGill, and Gerald D. Heilinga. *Aerospace: The Challenge.* Montgomery, Ala.: Civil Air Patrol, 1989.

Bolles, Richard N. *The 1989 What Color Is Your Parachute?* Berkeley, Calif.: Ten Speed Press, 1989.

Collegiate Aviation Directory: A Guide To College Level Aviation/Aerospace Study. Atlanta: Future Aviation Professionals of America, 1989.

Combs, Harry, and Martin Caidin. *Kill Devil Hill.* Boston: Houghton Mifflin, 1979.

Francis, Devon. *Mr. Piper and his Cubs.* Ames, Iowa: Iowa State University Press, 1973.

Gesell, Laurence E. *The Administration of Public Airports.* Chandler, Ariz.: Coast Aire Publications, 1988.

King, Frank H. *Aviation Maintenance Management.* Carbondale, Ill.: Southern Illinois University Press, 1985.

Loening, Grover. *Take Off into Greatness.* New York, N.Y.: G. P. Putnam's Sons, 1968.

NBAA Salary Survey (1988). Washington, D.C.: National Business Aircraft Association, 1988.

Taneja, Nawal K. *Introduction To Civil Aviation.* Lexington, Mass.: Lexington Books, 1989.

Wells, Alexander T. *Air Transportation: A Management Perspective.* Belmont, Calif.: Wadsworth Publishing Company, 1989.

Weisel, William E. *Spaceflight Dynamics.* New York, N.Y.: McGraw-Hill, 1989.